DEDICATION

Ronan dedication:

To Tony Cascarino, for goals and gas.

Lloyd dedication:

To Emma for being a constant source of inspiration,
Pompey for being a constant source of amusement, and
all those I am hastily forgetting in the acknowledgements.

Acknowledgements

Thanks to Matthew for belief in the project, and to Shell for laughing in all the right pages.

Additionally, the following made contributions to this book and we thank them, however bizarre their offering:

Professor Peter Wilkin and French Friends, Professor Rachel "Janice" Stone, Professor Joost Van Loon, Adam "Dougal" McLaughlin, James "it's oor oil" McLaughlin, Nathaniel Sikand-Youngs (almost certainly a Professor one day), Professor Tim Youngs (no, really) and Andy "Pineapple" Charles (certainly eccentric enough to be a Professor).

Testimonials (not real ones obviously)

'Great book on Euro 16. I think Brazil will win it!' - *Pele*

'Probably the best book on Euro 2016 - though I have included a six page letter on how I would make it better.' - *José Mourinho*

'No rush for a Brexit here, this is one Euro group we need to stay in!' - *Boris Johnson*

The incredibly helpful 'Should I buy this book?' persuasive factoids test thingy

(NB: If you have already bought this book, perhaps because you are a Fitzsimons completist, you liked the cover, or the price was right and your nephew's birthday was imminent, fear not, you have invested wisely. But if you've just furtively opened this in your local shop, please take our test to find out your suitability for purchase).

Did you know? (answer 'yes' or 'no')

1. Germany's win at Euro 96, as well as being extremely irritating, was also their very first at a major championship of any kind
2. They won whilst drinking more beer than any other nation in the tournament
3. You have more chance of winning Euromillions than Greece did of winning Euro 2004 in Portugal
4. France is the only nation to have won both the

European Championships and World Cup at home

5. We still can't believe Gascoigne didn't score an extra time golden goal in the European Championship semi-final of 1996

6. In previous tournaments Greece has refused to play Albania and Spain refused to play the USSR

7. Italy won a European Championship semi-final by coin toss

8. This book habitually refers to Scotland as 'Nonquallandia' (though this is far from the cheapest laugh it goes for)

Mostly YES: You want this book

Mostly NO: You NEED this book

Still not convinced?

Here are some amazing things which we were not able to include in the book, so imagine how fascinating it is!

a) Have UEFA taken the opportunity afforded by Michel Platini being on the naughty step to introduce goal line technology?

b) World Soccer's player of the year top 100 for 2015 includes Wales' Bale at 19, England's Rooney at 25 and Eire's Jon Walters at number 52.

c) In the above list, Richie Towell of the Republic and Dundalk is at 100, so why not a single Northern Irish player? We assume that Kyle Lafferty and Steven Davis were at numbers 2 and 3 between Messi and Ronaldo but somehow got accidentally excluded.

d) Just in case they make a late burst onto the scene let

us here mention Goncalo Guedes (Portugal), Benito Raman (Belgium), Lenny Nangis (France), Matias Nahuel and Sandro Ramirez (Spain) and Federico Bernadeschi (Italy) – coming soon on astronomical wages to the Premier League (possibly)

e) Albania's success is, in part, a result of the 1999 Kosovan War which spread Albanian refugees far and wide around Europe. Many of the current team have Kosovan roots.

f) Will weakness at full back force Philipp Lahm out of retirement in Germany?

g) Even more unlikely, will Adrian Mutu, erstwhile of Chelsea and Fiorentina and plagued by controversy, return from the Indian Super League (so called) to play for Romania aged 36?

h) Total capacity for all 10 stadiums is just shy of half a million (496,431) with the highest at St Denis (Paris) at 81,338) and the lowest in Toulouse at 33, 300.

i) Southampton beat Arsenal 4-0 on Boxing Day (2015) – although there are many other gratuitous mentions of things we like

So, as you can see, this is an absolutely essential purchase for any discerning football fan. And the rest of us as well. Enjoy your copy, enjoy the tournament, and here's to a home nation victory!

Euro 2016

The important Preface bit

Four English-speaking nations have qualified for Euro 2016. Blimey Charlie! How did that happen? So, before we launch into the vagaries of the authors' minds (which constitutes this guide), here's just a little about each of them to whet your whistle or some such nonsense. Dare you dare to dare to dream?

Dare to dream … Focus on England

Well, Greece were 150-1 to win the Euros in 2004. England are usually – realistically – about a 15-1 shot, so once every 60 years seems fair enough. If international football were the Premier League, England would usually finish in the top 10 and maybe qualify for the Champions' League. As well as winning the World Cup and almost reaching another final, we have actually been third in the Euros and in another agonising 1-1 semi-final draw, followed by penalties, against the Germans. It's not a bad record; there really aren't very many teams that have won the World Cup: 3 South American; 5 European if you group together wins by completely different Germanies.[1] Holland have not won the World Cup. Neither has Russia. The Czechs and Slovaks haven't, together or apart. Hungary failed to seize on their time as World's best team and Belgium are more likely to hold onto FIFA's number one spot than ever win the World Cup. Scotland haven't, though amazingly they were, once upon a time, very good. So we really haven't got so much to be ashamed of, but The Sex Pistols were surely right in 'God Save the Queen' to tell us that 'there's no future in England's dreaming'...

We simply have to let it go. We're not going to win it, but the hope is killing us. Lower your expectations. I don't know about you but I see players who seem like they could run forever in the Premier League look like they're carrying sacks of coal at major tournaments. Fear seems to provoke mis-controlled passes, hurried shots, hasty lunges and fumbling keepers; gone is the confidence and the playing without fear. All this seems to happen with the pulling on of the international shirt.

So please dare *not* to dream! Dare to imagine a festival of football in a country with many glorious culinary opportunities, lovely wine and ice cold beer that bites the next day (1664). Dare to imagine meeting people from all over Europe and sipping a friendly beer with them. Dare to imagine doing this without the need to sing songs about not surrendering to the IRA, nor the banality of '10 German bombers' being shot down by the RAF. What next? There were 10 Spanish galleons on the sea? Or 10 Viking longboats? Get our history of conquest and Empire in perspective and enjoy the bleedin' football, will you? It has to be less painful than thinking there's a chance surely?!

---

[1] See later for explanation of this very serious point.

Dare to dream ... Focus on Northern Ireland

There was actually a bit of a Twitter hashtag thing bearing this very title in the closing stages of the qualifying campaign, but this piece has nothing to do with that.

With a population of around 1.8 million (about 40% of that of the Republic), Northern Ireland has even fewer potential players to call upon than its neighbours to the south (and, the way the land lies, also to the west and the north).

In terms of World Cup history, the North eclipses the Republic by virtue of having reached the quarter-finals (or equivalent phase) twice: in 1958 and 1982. Neither co-author of this book was alive in 1958, but both got their homework finished early in 1982 to watch with eager anticipation as Northern Ireland – who had drawn their two earlier Group 5 games against Yugoslavia and Honduras – shaped up to face host nation Spain in Valencia. Spain were, at that time, not the powerhouse they have since become, but were on the ascendant and, let's not forget, were only two years away from securing the runner-up slot at Euro 1984.

Did Northern Ireland have a chance? George Best was long off the scene by this stage, but they had won the Home International Championship in 1980 (and were destined to do so again in 1984), so they were no slouches at a time when England were taken to be in their pomp, and Scotland had had a decent few years in terms of qualification for major tournaments. Both Spain and Northern Ireland needed a win to be absolutely certain of qualifying for the knockout stages, and the wise money was very much on the Spanish in front of a partisan crowd (and a Paraguayan referee). Against all the odds, and despite having a man sent off, the North held their own, and the mighty Gerry Armstrong capitalised on a goalkeeping mistake early in the second half to score the only goal of the game and send his side through as group winners.

What does this episode tell us? Aside from earning Armstrong a tasty transfer to Real Mallorca the following year, it tells us about the power of organisation, of not freezing on the big nights, of playing as a tight unit, and of taking your chances when they come along.

There are pleasing echoes of this spirit across the Celtic world as we approach Euro 2016. Look at what Wales and the Republic of Ireland have achieved. (And even though Scotland didn't qualify this time, there are seriously positive signs of progress under Gordon Strachan.) Together with Northern Ireland, these are all small nations in terms of population, pools of players to be drawn upon, and the relative obscurity of their national leagues (though giants compared to Iceland). It takes a particular brand of determination, organisation and national pride to blend a squad of (in effect) foreign-based players into a unit that can hold its own against supposedly much better opposition.

The boys also qualified for the 1986 World Cup in Mexico, but had the misfortune to be drawn in a group containing not only Spain but the mighty Brazil. Not the easiest of groups to think about getting out of, but they gave it their best shot. A better way to reflect on this is to have a look at the film *Shooting for Socrates* (released in 2014).

If 1982 and 1986 are too much like ancient history for you, maybe we could think about two glorious moments for Northern Ireland in the mid-noughties: a 1-0 victory over England in 2005 and a 3-2 smashing of Spain a year later. Not in friendlies, you understand: these were both high-profile qualifiers (the former for World Cup 2006, the latter for Euro 2008).

It can be done – this has been evident in the results discussed above, but also in the qualifying campaign for Euro 2016 under Michael O'Neill. Let's look at Group F. In principle, the only bone fide minnow was the Faroe Islands (though even they have started to pick off some cocky opponents, playing decent football and managing not to finish bottom of their group this time round). Greece have been royally and deservedly slagged off by my co-author for their comical fall from grace, after they had surprised him and everyone else by winning Euro 2004; but lining up in a group, you'd think they wouldn't be a pushover. The group also contained Romania and Hungary, historically both robust footballing nations and routine qualifiers for major tournaments, and Finland, who, despite never qualifying for the World Cup or European Championship finals, have always been a hard outfit to beat, particularly since their spell under the organisational eye of Roy Hodgson.

As it turned out, the North only lost one game: 2-0 to Romania in Bucharest. At all other times, they were fully in control, winning six matches and drawing three as they romped to first place in the group. This, to my mind, was nothing short of remarkable.

The squad in recent games has been packed with grafters who've learned a lot during their time playing in the English and Scottish leagues (plus Aaron Hughes in Australia). Even though we can see that there are players turning out for Hartlepool United, Doncaster Rovers, Notts County and

Fleetwood Town, we also know that they've developed – with Michael O'Neill's steady guidance and reassurance – a self-belief second to none. They're ready for action, and the dream is very much alive.

They'll be supported in vast numbers by the famed Green and White Army of travelling fans. This is no ordinary collection of football supporters; this is a brotherhood of soccer-mad fanatics from both sides of the religious coin, who have drawn international praise and awards for their focus on sport, on togetherness and on partying. *The Telegraph* reported in 2006 that Polish fans had applauded the Green and White army out of the stadium following their match in Warsaw.

From the team, from the fans, from the nation, expect tireless graft, relentless enthusiasm and exhaustive partying.

Bring it on – and dare to dream.

Dare to dream ... Focus on The Republic of Ireland

It's a special experience being a fan of the Republic of Ireland. The pressure is off. Fans support a team from a country of fewer than five million people, the sixth smallest of the 24 countries qualifying for the finals of Euro 2016. The entire squad plays abroad, and many of them were born and raised abroad. Do fans care? Maybe it would be preferable if the League of Ireland Premier Division were on a par with the English Premier League, but maybe not. Against all the odds, this small but proud nation looking out across the Atlantic has forged something unique in footballing terms.

We know the clichés: it's all about gauging expectations, rolling your sleeves up and playing your hearts out. But we also know that clichés are founded on an element – often a sizeable and unarguable element – of solid truth. Ireland doesn't do prima donnas. It works on the basis of getting a hardworking bunch of lads together whenever the complexities of the English, Scottish and American leagues allow it, and harnessing their pride and enthusiasm into a technically and organisationally sophisticated system.

We could look at recent history. Not many teams sharing a qualifying group with Germany manage to draw 1-1 with them away (take a bow, John O'Shea) and beat them 1-0 at home (join him, Shane Long). In fact, being paired with Poland and Germany in a group from which only two nations qualify automatically would send shivers down the spines of most people – but not the Irish. Martin O'Neill's men have shone at all levels in qualification – holding and beating the best, bossing countries considered their equals, and doing demolition jobs on the weaker nations as required. And they've done so with spirit, with skill, with polish, and above all they've done it as a unified group.

We could look at less recent history. For many of us, 1988 isn't such a long time ago, and it certainly fits within the parameters of the modern game. It was also the year that marked the beginning of the Republic of Ireland making their mark on the international stage. That was the year Ray Houghton – bookmark that name for later – stepped up and scored the goal that sank England 1-0 in Group B of the tournament in West Germany. A glance at the Group B table shows the Republic in third place ahead of England, who flunked the entire show with three defeats and zero points. The two nations above the Irish – the Soviet Union and the Netherlands – met again in the final, the imperious latter crushing the flailing former. But look more closely:

Ireland were only one point behind Holland in the group.

Something magical was afoot, and it came in the shape of hordes of happy, green-clad fans delighting in travelling to a major tournament for the first time ever. Make no mistake: this was no En-ger-land-style invasion of the meatheads; this was pure joy, smiley fraternity and an instinctive sharing of the craic across the European footballing community; this was hugs and beer – progression to the knockout stages would have been grand, but it wasn't to be, and that was fine.

It was to be, however, a mere two years later, and on an even bigger stage: Italia 90. It seems cruel in hindsight that so much attention was heaped on Gazza – who seized the tournament by its throat and was almost singlehandedly instrumental in getting England as far as they did, until the tears – when another unbelievable narrative was developing in Cagliari and Palermo. Ireland held England (the eventual winners of Group F) 1-1, with a goal from Kevin Sheedy, and after two more draws secured second place in the group. The subsequent round-of-16 tie against Romania has gone down in folklore – many a VHS tape has worn out with constant repetition of Packie Bonner's save and the improbable figure of David O'Leary stepping up to slot home the winning penalty in an unforgettable 5-4 shoot-out victory. This was what the fans wanted – not just an undreamt-of progression to the quarter-finals of the World Cup, but also a glorious stay of alcoholic execution as campsite and hotel extensions were hastily and affably negotiated with obliging Italian proprietors. An extra game; an extra party. OK, so the dream ended by the narrowest of margins against hosts Italy in the quarters, but where's the shame in that?

Let's dream. The facts were there in green and white, but

the experience was bigger than that. OK, the Irish had some exceptional players in their team, but what galvanised them was a togetherness and a work ethic similar to the one we see now in 2016. If you want any further evidence on the power of dreaming and the heights that can be reached, have a look at the film *The Van*, based on Roddy Doyle's novel.

We could go on. World Cup 1994 in the USA, and Ray Houghton destroying the mighty Italy in Group E; another progression to the knockout stages, with a loss to a still-powerful Dutch side. Keep dreaming. 2002 in Japan and South Korea saw the Irish finish second in Group E behind eventual finalists Germany, whom they held 1-1 in Ibaraki. Another fiercely contested draw in the last 16 saw Ireland hold Spain for 120 minutes, before losing on penalties.

What I'm saying here is that yes, they had a good squad, but the Irish were stronger than the sum of their parts. Importantly, wherever they went, legions of fans rocked up, sang their hearts out, hugged everyone they could and collapsed in a smiling, drunken stupor at the end of each game.

It's not all been this good, of course. We can cast our minds back to November 2009, when the Republic were paired up with France in the play-offs to reach the finals of the 2010 World Cup in South Africa. The boys had finished second behind Italy in their qualifying group, and had remained unbeaten in the campaign's ten games. They lost the first leg 1-0 in Dublin, but a Robbie Keane goal at the Stade de France propelled the Irish into extra time and gave them – once again – the right to dream, to dream of the tantalisingly tangible. Then up popped Thierry Henry with his crafty yet outrageous handball in the build-up to William Gallas's winner. Another dream shattered, but who was to say that the Irish weren't still more than holding their own among the best in the world? Eight of the Irish squad from that fateful day are also still very much in the running in the lead-up to Euro 2016.

It's not just about the big names. It's about spirit, teamwork and graft, and the Irish have this in spades. They aren't cowed by the big occasion, and the bigger the occasion, the bigger the party their loyal army of fans will create. What's to stop something memorable happening in 2016? Let's dare to dream...

Dare to dream ... Focus on Wales

The obvious reason to dream is that Wales have a secret weapon which none of the other countries can quite match. I refer, of course, to terrifying male close harmony singing. If you ever get the chance to listen to a scratchy recording of the pre-match singing at the 1927 Cup Final (won by Cardiff City) you will realise that, despite being favourites and then blaming the new shiny shirt of their goalkeeper, Arsenal never stood a chance against 'Land of My Fathers' delivered with a rarely heard 'from-the-heart passion'. So, Welsh fans, destiny is in your own hands, or rather mouths; show up in sufficient numbers and watch 'Deutschland über alles' and every other song tremble and die on the lips! Behind such singing, victory surely has a chance?

But if lusty baritones are Wales' secret weapon, then there is the not so secret weapon that is Gareth Bale. Initially played at Southampton as a left back, it took someone other than the grim managers Saints had at the time to realise that he was an outstanding attacking midfield player. One wonders how widely his reputation in the EPL as a 'diving little cheat' is known about; if it is, he could be in for a bit of a kicking, but if referees give him some protection he could just win the thing. Maradona was once the only decent player dragging Argentina to tournament success and it is possible that Bale can do the same for Wales.

Of course if you ask Gareth, or manager Chris Coleman, they will alert you to team spirit and insist that it's a team game and that Wales is more than a one-man team. Certainly organisation and hard work can go a long way in international football these days, but the reason Wales' odds of winning will be considerably lower than Albania's is that Wales have a world-class player. That said, are there any other reasons to be optimistic within the squad? In a word, yes!

First and foremost is that Wales does have some other very good players and others with potential. Ramsey, of course, can be an extremely effective goal-scoring midfielder when fit, and Joe Allen seems finally to be finding his feet at Liverpool. Up front, Sam Vokes is the one player who (if free from injury) might prove to have lots of potential. At the back Williams usually looks assured, as does Gunter. In goal Hennessey may not be perfect but he has bags of international experience and will – however good a job Pardew is doing – get a season of Premier League practice at Crystal Palace.

This lot combined played Belgium when Belgium was ranked 2 in the FIFA rankings and drew 0-0. They then played them when Belgium were 1 in the rankings and won 1-0, ferocious bouts of 'Land of My Fathers' seeing the boyos over the line. So why not dream? That said, in a feature for the BBC, previously injured squad hopeful Jack Collison puts his finger on the real reason for daring to dream. And that is the one that all countries – including Albania – will use, namely: 'if Greece can win it anyone can win it'. And Greece did it with little more than a Werder Bremen bit-part player up front, a goalkeeper who looked like George Clooney and a German coach.

If it's difficult to make a compelling case for a Welsh victory, it's also difficult to see many teams putting lots of goals past them. And whilst the ferocity of singing may not seem like a particularly potent weapon, one imagines that having not attended a major tournament since 1958, and with France so close, there will be amazing travelling support and that the singing really will be spine-tingling.

Dare to dream ... Focus on Scotland

Err, no! Tee hee!!

Hop on the ferry (a proper introduction)[1]

[Warning: This book is not entirely serious and shouldn't be taken too seriously. It is penned with the idea that it might act as a humorous lightweight accompaniment to the championships. As such it feels free to go off on ridiculous tangents and include material simply because it tickles the authors. Such a caveat notwithstanding, you will find sections on the history of the Euros, the qualifying campaign and the teams who have qualified, maybe even including official UEFA co-efficients if you're very good. It does have the details of when and where matches will be played and is an inexpensive gift for that special person in your life or the un-special person you wish to curry favour with. It can also be used

---

[1] This book really needed no introduction, and would have been better without this one probably. The title of the introduction would have been the title of the book if it weren't for the publisher's singular lack of imagination which he regards as 'market savvy'!

for taunting Scots. This is rather a long-winded way of saying that if you're one of those people who doesn't simply judge a book by the cover and actually starts reading it before deciding upon purchase, then go and buy it. You won't regret it for a second.][2],[3]

Writing in 2003 for a similar type of book was in many ways much simpler, and not only because I wasn't joined by an exceptionally witty co-author (Mr Fitzsimons) telling me that I'm not funny and wouldn't recognise funny if it bit me. It was also simpler because no English-speaking countries, except Eng-er-land, ever even looked like qualifying and so I wrote with a certain assurance that my readership, whilst undoubtedly as sophisticated as you are, was probably almost exclusively English and could nonetheless be relied upon to snigger, chortle or at the very least ignore my attempts to get cheap laughs by mentioning Costa Rica, Iran and Peru, or always suffixing Northern Ireland with the word 'nil' and other such hilarious literary devices, at the expense of British neighbours. You see, I can't help myself; I'm already repeating myself within seconds of the 'kick off' of this first foray into such a book since that ill-fated product of 2004. But anyway, at the time of starting writing this book (May 2015), I have to contend with the distinct possibility of a Welsh and Northern Irish readership (possibly even Scottish, although I really, really doubt it)[4] and so I will maintain respectful neutrality, at least until

---

[2] Warning: Period of regret is likely to exceed 1 second; always read the label.

[3] Further warning: One author is married to a Manchester United fan; the other not. One cricket fan, one not. One Eire-phile, one Republic-o-phobe. Confused? You might be.

[4] Call me Nostrodamus! (October 2015)

any of them is unable to qualify (when I will gleefully return to the needling).

"But wait!" I hear you exclaim as one mass of football (aka "fitba" in Non-Qualification-Landia) mad Britishness (because I still don't plan on being nice to the Republic's Pompey-esque pub team)[5] "what *was* so ill-fated about your guide to Portugal 2004?" Well, since you ask... sometime back in late 2003, I turned on my steam-powered PC and thought to myself: "Now what the f*** can I write about perennial no-hopers Greece?" after a few seconds contemplating some nice holidays and Greece's woeful football team I went for an approach in which cheese pies and Mythos beer emerged, it must be said, with a great deal of credit, but retsina and Greek football not so much. If it was simply 'eliminated at the group stage' I had committed to print, it might not have been so bad, since that was conventional wisdom. However, I went instead for a merciless tirade of satirical 'wit' and concluded that Greece had a snowball's chance in hell of actually winning Euro2004 in Portugal. The book went to print (acknowledging on the sleeve-notes some 'downright foolhardy predictions') and Greece became the most unlikely tournament winners ever, probably even including Denmark who won despite not even qualifying in 1992. In fact, foolhardy though my predictions might have been, Greece's pre-tournament odds were 150-1 for a tournament held every 4 years; that makes Greece's win a maximum once-every-600-year event!

Now, the Greek Orthodox Church don't do fatwas, but I was genuinely surprised only to receive the one death

---

[5] Only joking, Martin O'Neill doing a splendid job etc etc

threat, and even that turned out to be a spoof (oh how I laughed!). Nonetheless, reputation in tatters, I retreated from my keyboard vowing never to write about football again.[6] However, salvation of sorts arrived in 2014 with Germany's 7-1 World Cup semi-final demolition of an inept and embarrassing Brazil, playing in a home World Cup. Brazil was coached by Luiz Felipe Scolari, the very same fellow who coached Portugal when they lost *twice* to Greece in 2004, including the final, and despite hosting the tournament. At last I had a scapegoat; it was not an awful prediction, it was all Big Phil's fault. And so, with a co-author to share the blame this time, I agreed to give it another go. The results you hold in your hand, doubtless with some trepidation after such a waffly opening page or two.

So, this is a book which is not so much a guide (although that's what it claims) as a series of words which are, at times, vaguely related to the topic. It is as much a product of its two authors' (and a number of contributors') desires to be stand-up comedians as anything else; the fact that they are writing books is a reflection of how just how 'good' their stand-up comedy is. To prove a point:

My very best joke

A duck waddles into a pub and says, "Can I have a pint of bitter please?"

---

[6] Unless you include my best-selling biography of Matthew Le Tissier, *One Man Team*, which was originally published in 2005 and is now available through Urbane. By 'best-selling' I mean compared to my co-authored pedagogical extravaganza about teaching using the internet called *Untangled Web* (Pearson, 1999) which generates reminders of the unearned advance to this day.

"Certainly, sir," says the barman, "that'll be £3.50."

To which the duck replies, "Could you just pop it on my *bill*?" [chuckle]

Then the duck says, "Do you sell condoms?"

"Yes, they're £2," says the barman, "and I suppose you'd like that putting on your bill too?"

"What kind of pervert do you take me for!?" says the duck. [laugh] The End

My Co-Author's best joke

A man walks into a pub with a giraffe. They spend all night drinking heavily, and as they go to leave the giraffe falls unconscious to the floor.

"Oi!" says the barman to the man, "you can't leave that lyin' 'ere."

"Snot a lion," slurs the man, "iss a graffe." The End

When I say my best joke, there is also the one about pigeons taking over the Philippines – they're calling it the coup of the century. Coo? Pigeon? No? Well anyway, what *will* you find within these pages if not rib-tickling humour...

- At least one fact about every team which is so geeky that it guarantees no second dates with that person you met through internet dating and are afraid likes you

- A witty sociological piece on why the French will never understand the English (British this time?) obsession with football

- Enough information on each host city to make the purchase of a Lonely Planet guide extremely recommended

- A witty historical essay on why cricket might be a much better bet (although this had to be deleted due to a lack of cricketing and historical knowledge, oh and indeed wit, and then reinserted to boost the word count, and then deleted because it's a non-sensical argument and then...well you'll just have to see if it's in or not)

- Useful French phrases translated, such as: 'your father was a hamster and your mother smelled of elderberries', 'good afternoon, I'm the Lord Mayor of Rotherham...no, not *Rozzer'am*' and 'good appetite'

So to achieve these lofty aims, as alluded to earlier, and in what can only be described as a cunning stunt, I will this time be accompanied by the master of all puns and Spoonerisms, the equally weighty Mr Ronan Fitzsimons. Together we have compiled, with nothing more than a cheeky smile and a flair for waffle, what people are already calling 'a pile of old tosh which made me titter a bit...occasionally...well, I'd had a few'. And who will we slag endlessly in the hope of a 'Greece-effect' this time? Well not England for sure, because they're absolutely shit and have no chance whatsoever!

It is said of a good introduction that it does none of the things this book has done so far. But since I've begun in a manner which suggests I've just got in from the pub and can't string a coherent sentence together, I'll continue just as long as this half a bottle of red lasts or until it causes me to fall asleep on the keyboar... uuuuuuuuuuuuijhy.

For those of you wondering, that was what happens if you're stone cold sober and pretend to fall asleep on your keyboard by gently head-butting it. Of course I'm not drunk! You deserve better. No, really, you all deserve much, much better. So anyway, I was wondering, if '50 years of hurt', 'the virtues of Englishness' and a gentle mocking of our island neighbours couldn't be the unifying theme of this book (because some of them qualified), then what might be? What is it (I asked myself earnestly) which unites football fans in Derry, Stranraer, Colwyn Bay and Workington? Well, alright I'll grant you, a certain oddness, extra digits and funny voices but that's not *really* what I was getting at. And yes, I'll grant you, you're all also united in outrage that you're over 1000 words into this so called 'guide' and you're as near to finding out about the championships as someone who's been reading Barbara Cartland novels or digging the garden.

But it did occur to me that there are probably more people in the UK as a whole who hate Manchester United than support England. And probably more English premiership managers than people who think Fabian Delph is an international footballer. So, in unbelievably random fashion, here's something for you all. Manchester United fans, and indeed football fans, oh and people, are advised to ignore this next boxed section...

Football United: Stand up if you hate Man U

Author's note: Payments for the book on Euro 2004 were 'vast'. So vast that I couldn't be arsed to do another one for over a decade. Anyway, they were just about 'vast' enough for a brief jaunt to the tournament itself, to take in classics such as Spain v (oh surely not, good god, really, really, how did they win it?) Greece and Denmark v Bulgaria. I travelled with 4 others who supported Leeds, Luton, Norwich and Liverpool respectively. Having decided who would drive (and boy did we get that wrong, but that's another story) we needed to decide upon the official tour T-shirt. In the end we went with simplicity meets populism. On the front the badges of the above teams, plus mine, the mighty Saints, Southampton. On the back the simple legend, "Stand Up if you hate Man U" (except in Portuguese). These proved tremendously popular, although created havoc on the journey out; having consumed a few ales prior to departure, and seated at the front of the plane, we were frequently getting up to visit the toilet, each time causing a fuselage -length Mexican wave of appreciation and endorsement. In fact, if you take the British Isles as a whole, "ABU" (ANYONE but United) probably unites more footy fans than any other single thing about football. This includes supporting England, loathing the referee and eating pies. Anyway, imagine (if you can) the outright horror of one day waking up to find yourself married to a fan of Satan's own team. It makes the 'we've come on holiday by mistake' moment in *Withnail and I* seem like a mere bagatelle! Anyway, it happened to Janice (we've changed that from her real name, Rachel, to hide her blushes) ... and as part of her therapy, because she's been declared clinically insane, interviewed her for our little book. Unless you actually support the (insert expletive here),[1] please enjoy and know that this is an important part of this unfortunate woman's recovery.

Author: How romantic are Man U fans then, Rach ... I mean Janice?

Janice: Our married life started with a journey in the back of his uncle's car, which was covered in dog hair, at about 1.30am, because he was too tight to get a taxi back to our house and too drunk to walk. So arriving exhausted, smelling of damp collie and in the early hours I stepped across the threshold hauling a pissed husband.

Author: But surely things got better? Err...I can tell by that hideous grin that they didn't...was there anything in particular you found it difficult to endure?

Janice: You mean apart from the extremely perverse sexual practices?

Author: Yes, apart from those, we're hoping for a PG certificate...

---

[1] But really, it is only football....even if some Man U fans are tremendously irritating.

Janice: Well mainly the celebrating; the pathetic gloating… having beaten Scunthorpe U11s 16-0 with a squad full of internationals I'd be subjected to endless wild whooping. It was nauseating. And having the 12 Days of Christmas chanted continuously with 'Cantona' inserted for each of the days' gifts ought to be a capital offence. I kid ye not, living with a United fan really is not a lovely experience in many ways.

Author (laddishly, though not endorsing lad culture): A bit of drinking, a bit of singing, a bit of adult sex play…surely it wasn't that bad? It doesn't sound *that* bad?

Janice: Mere moments after having given birth I was dragged from my hospital bed, the placenta still attached to me and my nearly born baby's belly button not yet tied; we were off to Old Trafford to go and seat my beautiful baby boy in Fergie's pitch-side seat. We didn't ever have our children christened as we don't believe in all that stuff but his forehead was marked with the mud from which the turf springs at Old Trafford. We also got to sit on a chair in the Red Café, which had Solskjaer's name neatly painted on the back, having paid about £4.50 for a cup of tea and a biscuit. What was I thinking?

[Editor's note: Whilst some readers might be disturbed by the foregoing, you'll be pleased to know that the young boy was unharmed and has gone on to lead a mercifully Man U-free existence][2]

Years following the birth of that first and then subsequent son contained many a weekend afternoon being abandoned

---

[2] In a further gesture towards those of a more sensitive disposition, the words 'behind every man in lycra there lies a total c***' were judiciously deleted from this piece, and then unfortunately and injudiciously added as this footnote.

with children and receiving an 'order' for dinner at 6pm. Then he didn't show up until 8pm, carrying a take-away, and accompanied by raucous mates. This was followed by an evening of washing up once he and the gang had left again for the pub and drinking utopia. Depression, funnily enough, soon followed along with a feeling of injustice, abandonment and complete boredom.

Author: So when did you realise it was over?

Janice: I paid £60 for a session with Relate. It was right at the end of my marriage; I wanted out. I was struggling to get him to listen to me so I booked a session with Relate. 'I don't love you,' said I, 'I want to leave this marriage.' So £60 later we started to talk, after the session, on the way back to our home. 'So husband, you see I need out of this, it is making me unhappy,' sayeth I unto the man to whom I had pledged myself. 'I cry myself to sleep because I am fed up with being a door mat; I see more of your dirty, sweaty sports kit than I do of you. You are always going out to the rugby, the football, anything that gets you out of the house and away from me and our children....' At which point I realised he was no longer listening and I ask myself actually, had he ever listened? In fact, I'd completely lost him physically as well as metaphorically. He had stopped outside the pub at the end of our road to peer in through the window to see what the football score was. The bastard. United had won. F****** b****** c****. The complete and utter f****** b******.

Author: So how are things now that he's no longer your husband?

Janice: [scoffs] Oh, now? Now?! He's only a b***** season ticket holder in lieu of paying a decent amount of child maintenance. Oh, sorry, the vitriolic poison that haunts my soul and is the reason for years of pyscho-analysis is beginning to seep out already. I knew it would and I have tried to keep it hidden but actually now the floodgates are breeched we might just as well get on with the sledging ... [and it went on and on and on and could easily have been a book in its own right but we had to stop. You get the point though – b*******]

Author's endnote: Rachel is recovering nicely. Thanks to your generosity in purchasing this book, a donation has been made and she has been placed with the Brothers of the Soil commune in Wales, England where she passes her day knitting jumpers out of her own armpit hair and stroking the beards of whichever brother takes her fancy. She has no access to Sky TV and a henna tat which says 'hate Man U' which never wears off because she doesn't wash.]

But don't worry, dear reader, it gets less random than this, if only because it couldn't get more so. And if you're tired of working through the ramblings of the inane and insane, just flip ahead and you'll find some guidey bits sure enough: history of the tournament, qualifying campaign, teams, host cities - that sort of usual guidey thing. But in this introduction, I wanted to offer you something different and compellingly useless. So, at absolutely no expense, I commissioned Professor Peter Wilkin, Head of Creative Interference at the Université de Lille, long-time Francophile but considered un sandwich short of a pique-nique by most of France, to gauge the opinion of the homme on the omnibus de Clapham (yeah, I know it doesn't really make any sense). This, for those of you who will travel, offers an insight into what to expect, and a warning that simply shouting louder, or even speaking French, will not necessarily make you understood. So, here are the Professor's not altogether surprising findings.

Do they mean us? A French take on English footballing obsession [3]

So here I am [Professor Pierre] surrounded by French football supporters in a bar near Nantes with only a slim and tentative grasp of the language. My mission: To offer you a guide to the French psyche. To break the ice, I decide to make a few humorous cultural observations.

Me: Do you know Monsieur Tourettes from *Modern Toss*? He's *f**king* hilarious! (thinking they would get the obvious swearing joke).

Silence (or 'Silence' (see-lonce) as it is in French)

Michel: Non, je ne connais pas M. Tourettes. C'est une comédie, peut-être? (No I don't, is that a comedy by any chance?)

Hmmmmmm, this isn't going to work, I thought, so I tried something less witty.

Me: I was driving near Tours the other day and passed a garage run by M. Georges Bastard [true]. I bet he does a *mean* MOT!

Jules: Vraiment? Pourquoi? (Really? Why's that?)

Clearly comedy is already a huge cultural division between

---

[3] For the purposes of this book that can be taken as 'British'

the French and the English – we do it and they don't. I mean, name me 5 famous French comedians. 4 even. 1 then. Apart from Jacques Tati. So I decide to press ahead with the football in order to dig the trench I've made a little deeper.

Me: So what do you think is the biggest difference between French supporters and English supporters?

Marcel: That is easy: the English are amazing. They go to every tournament and genuinely believe they have a chance of winning it, when in fact they have none. The French supporters go into every tournament with a team that might actually win it, but they don't believe it is possible, and so they don't.

Ah-hah, I thought, that sounded like a Gallic aphorism. Excellent. Let's press on.

Me: Why is that?

Marcel: It is the French way; we only support a winning team when it appears likely that the tide has turned in our favour.

Clement: It was exactly like that in the World Cup in 1998.

Me (helpfully): Oh, and with everyone pretending to have been in the resistance in WW2 rather than collaborating with the Nazis!?

Marcel: Non! That was *completely* different.
[Very awkward silence/'silence tres awkward'.]

Me: So do you think France can win the tournament this time as it is on home territory?

Erik (slapping the table): Non! Of course not! Something

will happen - the players will go on strike, the Italians will shaft us, the coach will be useless, everyone's trousers will fall down.[4] It is the French way.

Me: But what about England then? Can they win it?

Erik (as everyone laughs): Of course not! You will run about a lot, but very slowly. The ball will make fools of your players. It always does. It is like watching 5-year-olds trying to control a football. Or monkeys juggle a Sevres vase. I don't know why but that is how it looks. It always ends in disaster for the English.

Me (again trying to be helpful): So like at Dunkirk!?

Jean-Pierre: Non! That was not a disaster for the English, it was a disaster for France. You all ran away!

Me (moving on rapidement): Yes, quite, errr, if you could choose one English player for the French team, who would it be?

At this point they put their heads together to confer. After several minutes they looked up.

Erik (on behalf of France): We really like your Steven Gerrard...

I'm puzzled.

Me: Really? But he's 75 years old, retired in LA and as likely to be in the English squad as Morgan Schneiderlin...

Jules: But he is magnificent, so much energy, he never

---

[4] All part of the interview except this last one which is covered by the book's 'anything for a cheap laugh' clause which was clearly displayed in the small print at the point of sale.

stops running around, he can kick the ball a long way too, further than most goalkeepers in fact; he is like a little boy in the park. Not like our players, cynical greedy bastards like Evra, Benzema and Ribéry!

Me: But they are *great* players! Apart from Evra, of course...

Michel: Yes, perhaps that is it. We simply find it hard to love our players even when they are great.

Me (again trying to be helpful): Ah, so you mean like Platini? - Now he really is a fat little so-and-so!

All: Non! We all love Platini.

At which point I gave up with this contrary bunch and lapsed into a state of moderate refreshment via the traditional French route of red wine.]

The moral of this story: they simply don't think like us, so try not to do that thing where you just shout louder to get your point across. At this point, I suppose you'll be wanting to hear something about the championships for which this book acts as a supposed guide? Oh, go on then...

History of the European Championships

Isn't it quite extraordinary how unlike the French 'we' are? Turn on day-time TV or radio in this country (unless you really are reading this on the Eurostar just outside Lille, in which case I mean the UK) and it'll be some or other desperate domestic situation along the lines of "You beep! You beeped my beeping husband you beep. I'll beeping kill you, you beep - by sticking a beeping pineapple up your beeping beep!!"; or else it's something about football. But in France it's very different indeed; a panel discussing varieties of stuffed olives or which wine to serve with quail would be more usual. Or it might be something about the relevance of continental philosophy in everyday life. I dare say from a distance – let us say somewhere in Zimbabwe, the Democratic People's Republic of Korea or inside Islamic State – that we probably have much in common, but from here it can often be difficult to see that. We're just very different and it is more than language which makes us mutually incomprehensible.

And so not in any xenophobic way, I often think that without France being 'in the way' we'd be spending much more time celebrating our Europeanness; that take away France and we'd be much better friends with the rest. We'd all be sipping knee-tremblingly strong trappist ales, eating *much* bigger sausages and falling asleep under trees all afternoon, before drinking stronger coffee and going out to dinner at midnight with the kids. Well that's what I think. In fact, in the 2004 version of this book, I went on to 'diss' anything French, blaming them for England's inability ever to win the tournament and justifying the puerile stereotyping by claiming that it was good acclimatising stuff for what the papers would say during the tournament. Well, I was probably right about that, but here I don't intend to repeat the tosh from then. Nor shall I simply tell you what you can get from Wikipedia or World Soccer. No, here I intend to make up some entirely new and 'interesting' tosh on the basis of minutes of research and a warped imagination.

In summary: The European football championships are most notable for Gazza's goal against Scotland in 1996 and WEST Germany's (when it existed) defeat to Czechoslovakia (when it existed) twenty years earlier on penalties.

The first thing to say is that the European Championship record-keepers apparently make the same mistake that they do at the World Cup, and that is that anything West Germany won now seems to count as 'Germany' winning it. This is preposterous. Now my German friends don't like this argument, but it's like the home nations coming together as 'Great Britain and Northern Ireland (Nil)' and then saying that 'Great Britain and Northern Ireland (Nil)' won the World Cup in 1966. They clearly didn't, we wouldn't say that, and neither did 'Germany' win Italia 90. It's like me saying Andy Murray was the first Englishman to win Wimbledon since the war. It's just wrong. And allow me to correct that wrongness right now by cheering you up and telling you that Germany's win in 2014 was therefore their *first* World Cup win (Germany uniting in November 1990 after the West Germans' rather lucky win in Italia 90). So 48 years *after* England beat them so convincingly at Wembley the Germans finally won the thing. Well done them. So we'll call that 1-1 then? Pass me the straws, please, I feel in need of a clutch at them.

And if you think 'we' have a problem with the Germans, just see what the Dutch have to say:

No matter what sport, it is always a highlight for the Dutch when they beat the Germans, which by the way is not as easy as it sounds, since there are 5 times more Germans than Dutch and they are good at almost every sport that they do (apart from Korfball). However, nowhere is the urge to win greater than with football. "Our 1966-moment" was 8 years after 1966, when the finals of the World Cup were held in West Germany and the Dutch were – for the first time in their, until then, rather pathetic football history – actually much better than their neighbours on the east side. Whereas the West Germans were struggling, the Dutch were flying through the group stages, humiliating big footballing nations such as Brazil and Argentina on the way.

But then after scoring a penalty within the first minutes, and without the West Germans having even touched the ball, it all went wrong. Twice Gerd Müller struck and left a nation weeping. It was not until the semi-finals of the European Championships of 1988, ironically again in West Germany, when we beat them 2-1 and partied for weeks, that this perennial injury could be somewhat alleviated.

This kind of dislike is mutual; I hasten to add. Ask any average German football lover which country they hate losing to most and they will unequivocally refer to "die Niederlande". We call them arrogant and they call us arrogant, probably because most of us really are. However, since about the turn of the Millennium, Germany has also by and large imported the Dutch youth academy system and as a result now probably has the strongest general youth development programme, second only to Spain. As much as the Germans are our biggest rivals, we seem unable to stop helping them get the better of us even more.

The Dutch not only think the Germans are arrogant, they also dislike them because they are so successful, so determined, so precise, so rational, so pünktlich, and because the grammar of their language is so unnecessarily systematic and complicated. The hardest thing is watching the German national football team win and they usually do, like at the World Cup in 2014, especially in the semi-finals against Brazil. We, the Dutch, felt the pain of the entire nation of Brazil in every fibre of our being, in every meme of our cultural existence; it hurt so much every time the ball went in.

Then, in the final, the pain of seeing Gonzalo Higuaín fail again and again as he faced the ultimate embodiment of what we dislike about the Germans, Manuel Neuer, on his own, was almost as unbearable, only to be topped by Mario Götze's lucky punch during extra time. The only thing in which the Dutch clearly outshine the Germans regarding football is suffering. The German national football team does not really know what suffering is. Losing 5-1 at home to England might have been the closest experience of it, but sure enough they bounced back immediately thereafter. It is above all for that reason, we hate the Germans almost as much as we love ourselves.

Gert van Ass – real Dutch name and not a matter for sniggering [1]

OK, that first bit was, as you'll have realised, not tosh at all, but cold hard reasoning. But the tosh is on its way, fear not, as I take you down memory lane, given that nearly the whole thing has been entirely forgettable.

A Frenchman first had the idea of holding the tournament in 1927 and, once he'd got his trousers up and fastened, the first tournament got underway in 1958 [Editor's Note: OK consider that a yellow card for crass cultural stereotyping; it's not big and it's not clever and that's about seven minor offences already]. The finals in France in 1960 had just 4 teams remaining from 17 entries, which did not include England, with WEST Germany, Italy and Holland all also eschewing the tournament at this early stage. In an age when the USA will play Iran, for example, and all manner of genocidal lunacy can be ignored in order to play football, the whole enterprise is perhaps most notable for Spain, then a model of authoritarian poverty, entrenched privilege and treading on 'the people' under Franco, refusing to play its quarter-final against the USSR on the grounds that the USSR was a country which believed in an entirely different system of authoritarian poverty, entrenched privilege and treading on 'the people'. In the

---

[1] It's reassuring for the Dutch to know that they won't lose to Germany in Euro 2016. This is one of our more robust predictions.

final the USSR (which no longer exists) beat Yugoslavia (which also no longer exists) 2-1 (which does still exist). And you see that just proves my point about 'West Germany' not being the same as 'Germany'. I mean people don't go around saying that the 1960 European Championship final was Latvia 2 Montenegro 1 just because the former was then in the USSR and the latter was part of Yugoslavia. Different countries! Now get 3 of those world cup stars off your shirts this instant, Germany! I shall keep on about this until somebody listens mind you ...

Moving on (but not for long!) the four who qualified for the 1964 finals had been whittled down from 29 entries. Whether these included any of the home nations I haven't bothered to look up, although frankly since they didn't appear in the finals, I'm assuming England did not. Oddly, this time it was Greece getting on the political high horse, withdrawing after drawing Albania with whom they were at war. Spain (playing in Madrid) managed to swallow their pride and take the field with the USSR this time and beat them 2-1 in the final. For the next tournament in Italy in 1968, 31 teams entered; according to Wikipedia (quoting UEFA) this was a 'testament to its burgeoning popularity' although that seems extremely unlikely, does it not? Italy beat the USSR by 'coin toss' in the semi-final after a draw. The final was also a draw but settled by a replay rather than tossing. Had the Italians lost their 'special' coin? In terms of tossing, did they feel Yugoslavian communism presented a bigger challenge than that of the Soviet Union? Was Tito a bigger tosser than Brezhnev? These are trivial questions which serious football historians rightly ignore to this very day. England in any case proved they were the best team in

Europe; having unluckily lost to Yugoslavia, they thrashed the USSR 2-0 without the aid of a coin to claim a never bettered third place. Frankly though, having surveyed the first decade of the championships, the real question (answered below) is why bother to play football in the summer anyway?

It's simply not cricket (or why cricket is better than football)

I successively asked 3 renowned brain-boxes and cricket-o-philes to write this piece and in the end everyone had an excuse, despite there apparently being 101 reasons why cricket is better than football. So, I guess you'll have to assume that football is, after all, the better game, although I've attempted 5 reasons for the opposite view, just to show willing:

- There are usually cakes at cricket
- There's often less swearing
- It's easier to 'work from home' at the cricket
- There are probably marginally more wickets per hour at cricket than goals at football
- Manchester United do not play cricket

But no, and lo, in the nick of time comes some eloquence that the book was otherwise much lacking!

The game of football; the life of cricket.

The roar of the crowd was a ceaseless song of devotion to the rhythm of play. It rose and fell, but never once paused, as the balance of the game swung to and fro. At the moment of kick off, the match seized your imagination and captured your heart, carrying you with a relentless grip right up until the final whistle blew. Here, it dropped you. The match ended, and you and your sporting compatriots were left stranded facing an unkind reality: England, knocked out, again. Euro 2016 — a glory that will be won by another nation. What a cruel world; how fruitless your love!

At its idyllic best, free from the interruptions of ludicrous dives, reckless tackles, and unattractive clearances out of the field, football is a continuous, fluid sport. It does not stop to catch its breath, and neither can those watching. How appealing, how exhilarating, how *beautiful* this all makes football, you probably think. Perhaps this is true. But to possess these qualities, a fleeting game of football sacrifices certain virtues which can only come from a longer passage of time. For a sport like a slow burning candle, unfolding in a sweeping landscape with a rhythm that breathes not races, take a seat at the pavilion end and relish in cricket.

Structurally, cricket is simply the cyclical repetition of the same formulaic "units" of play. The bowler pryingly delivers a ball of cork and leather; the batsman answers with a blade of willow. Repeat: six times. Over. Repeat: twenty, fifty, maybe more, times. Innings. Teams swap. Repeat: from the top. For those only familiar with football, this structure can seem disjointed, impenetrable and, the word most commonly used, *boring*. Each ball bowled is a singular occasion, distinct and autonomous from the deliveries that came before. In football, every pass and touch of the ball is wholly dependent on the outcome of the preceding events. The only continuity in cricket, nay, the only evidence that any play actually took place before the current moment, is in the number of runs scored and wickets taken, the wear of the players' minds, and the tear in the ball and pitch. These amount to the sporting symbols of: human imperatives of measurement, understanding, and narrative-writing; human capabilities of psychological and physical endurance; and human helplessness to the environment and the passing of time.

Cricket is no less than life itself played out over twenty-two yards. As such, the spectator who is bored of cricket is bored of life. No matter what the balance of the game, we cannot predict what the next delivery will bring. The strongest innings can crumble in a fraction of a session, while the weakest need only a sturdy partnership to erode away the time left in the day's play. Either way, one team will be left mourning the ruins of its once dominant positon, just as human beings are so often left feeling powerless to determine their own destinies. Of course, fates twist and fortunes exchange in football, too, but the fluid structure of the sport means that such game-changing moments always come out of somewhere even if they are unpredictable. The losing team in football still has to set up that pivotal surprise goal, whereas the underdog fielding side in cricket can produce a wicket from nowhere. Most of all, cricket pauses, composes itself, and walks back to its bowler's mark, affording the spectator the chance to absorb the full enormity of these junctures in a game.

So, by the time that England[2] have lost in Euro 2016 and the brief excitement and enchantment of that game of football has passed, turn over to the cricket. From one ball to the next, it will show you joy, monotony, surprise, defeat and success, all in a day's play.

Some essential facts

The two European Championships finals held in the 1970s were between countries that no longer exist. West Germany (three time winners of the World Cup incidentally before no longer existing!) beat the USSR in 1972 (in Belgium) and Czechoslovakia beat West Germany in 1976 5-3 on penalties in Yugoslavia. Now the Germans claim that Germany won it in 1972 (even though it was West Germany), but neither the Slovaks nor the Czechs claim to have won in 1976, although perhaps that's because it took place in a country that doesn't exist, or they were embarrassed by being 2 countries against a half a country? But, as George puts it in Blackadder, it all seems to me like another case of the vile Hun and his villainous empire building. Well it's nothing like that at all actually, but I am bringing to bear the same level of robust argument. Worth mentioning again the winning penalty by the Czechs; one of those little dinks down the centre, except unlike when Gary Lineker tried it the goal-keeper dived.

In 1980, as a novelty, a country which still exists (although somewhat grumpily it must be said) actually reached the final; Belgium losing to WEST Germany 1-2. In a new format, the winners of groups of four teams played the final.

---

[2] ..and Wales, and Northern Ireland, and the Republic of Ireland...

England's first game of the tournament was a 1-1 draw against Belgium – not bad in historical terms, but entirely over-shadowed by a press reaction which suggested we were more of a pub team than internationals. And that was further over-shadowed by English football hooligans coming up against Italian riot police (Italian riot police are so called because of their ability to start riots at will).[3]

France, who like England, **Germany** *and* Spain have won the World Cup once (and *only* **once**), won their first major tournament at home in 1984. They beat Spain in the final and Platini did jolly well. And in 1988 Holland beat West Germany including Marco Van Basten's incredible volleyed goal from an acute angle. In 1992 the run of teams who still exist winning the tournament was extended, as warring, soon to not exist (like West Germany), Yugoslavia was expelled and the Danes (who had not originally qualified) left the beach and cruised to victory. In the final they beat Germany, so it was the arch Europeans [4] against the Euro-sceptics and much to everyone's delight the Germans lost; some commentators had described them as 'current World Champions', but as you know by now, they were playing in their first tournament for a very long time. Does it seem like the heart has gone out of this history? It feels very much like that to me...notwithstanding my undimmed enthusiasm for the 'Germany's only won one world cup' argument which I may have ever so slightly over-done?

---

[3] An insight into the enlightened methods of Italian police can be gleaned from Tim Parks' *A Season with Verona*, London: Vintage, 2003. It's also a proper football book, if such things are of interest.

[4] If you slow it down and play it backwards, the German tournament song says "We're all German now! Did we say German? Err, that's just our crazy sense of humour...we mean we're all European now... obviously...ho ho!"

I think the reason for my declining enthusiasm for this section is that it all takes me back to 1996. I was 30, going on 17. Very rarely drunk, but very rarely sober. Baddiel and Skinner's *Football's Coming Home* played from every jukebox in England; Psycho (Stuart Pearce) scored a penalty in a shoot-out to win against Spain, thus burying the ghost (or so we thought) of Italia 90; the sun shone and I drank beer. And then one midweek night, somewhere near Fulham, I watched in a pub as England out-played Germany in the Euro semi-final, ought to have won in normal time, nearly scored a golden goal in extra-time through Gasgoigne and even scored all their 5 penalties for the second shoot-out in a row – and *still* lost to Germany – although of course, we'd never lost to Germany on penalties before (assuming you're following the over-done argument above!). And I mean Germany; fully united and no chance of claiming it was a different country. Kunz! Kunz scored Germany's equaliser and from then on it was painful, right down to watching the news next morning and discovering that some of my fellow countryman had not taken the news lying down (comatose) as I had, but had rioted and torched German cars etc. WTF? FFS! Germany went on to win the final against another new country, the Czech Republic. I was there. Was I also the only one to notice that the linesman originally put his flag up for offside, but then put it down amid the golden goal celebrations? Maybe I imagined it. In any case, I was grudging at best.

Actually, I was angry anyway. That summer began with my 'Brazil Would Pick Le Tiss' banner getting some decent media coverage, as England lost 1-3 at the old Wembley to the Brazilians. Terry Venables continued to ignore Le Tiss, although that may have been as much to do with Le Tissier's non-move to Spurs earlier in the decade during which he had apparently ignored a phone call from Terry. In any case, by the Germany game I had got over that, although defeat brought it to the surface again. What am I trying to say? Mainly that for me the relevant 'History of the European Championships' is a very brief period in between June and July 1996. All else is irrelevant and available on Wikipedia. Just go will you...leave me alone!

[Sometime later, I sulkily return to the keyboard]

France won in 2000. Greece somehow in 2004 (next due a win in 2604 at the earliest). Spain in 2008 and 2012, thus becoming the first team to successfully defend the Euro, sandwiching their 2010 World Cup win. You're probably old enough to remember it all anyway, so hardly worth bothering you with it. It will take something *totally* unexpected in 2016 to revive my enthusiasm.

2016:
The Qualifying Campaign

Half Time

At the time of writing, something totally unexpected may be about to happen; that being the qualification of more than one 'home nation' for the finals. England look likely to qualify and easily for once, which is why I'm writing anything at all at this stage, because only English qualification activates the enormously lucrative 'cash for tosh' contract that we have negotiated. But, there is more than that. Guided by Steven Davis of Southampton, Northern Ireland have shaken off the 'nil' tag/gag and might even qualify; granted, their win in Athens may look less impressive in the light of the Faroe Islands winning there too, but they are going well with 4 wins from 5 and in second place to Romania at the halfway stage (Yes, little more than a decade on from winning in Portugal, Greece lost at home to the Faroe Islands in a competitive match!).[1]

---

[1] And away too!!!

Wales are similarly finding a way to win – as unimpressively in Andorra as impressively in Israel - but they are winning and trailed Belgium only on goal difference at the halfway stage. And even the perpetual no-hopers of international football (Scotland, who else?) in a particularly tough group are showing signs that they might just squeak into the finals, at the halfway stage just a point behind Poland, level with Germany and ahead of the Republic of Ireland. If you don't know who qualified, read on; at the moment of penning these words I don't know either.

Group A

I can remember my outrage when Southampton had 73% of possession at home to Aston Villa but nonetheless managed to lose 2-3. But they say international football is just that next step up, so 'well played' to World Cup wizards Holland for having 74% of possession and yet losing 2-0 in Reykjavik to Iceland. Indeed, after also losing to the Czech Republic, Holland got off to a terrible start in this group, which was headed at the halfway stage by the Czechs and Icelanders. I know it's a bit of a tangent, but no one would ever go to Ice Land for some winter sun would they? I was just wondering what other countries would be called if their names were such obviously descriptive warnings? Belgium already styles itself 'Beer Land' for instance. But that's a game I'll leave to you, because I'm already on a yellow card from the publisher for crass cultural stereotyping![2] Where was I? Oh yes, Holland/terrible start/even losing at home to Kazakhstan with half an hour left etc etc.

---

[2] Not that that seems to have put him off – publisher.

With shock qualifications looking likely all over the place, Iceland's 2-1 win v the Czechs, having trailed 0-1, made their progress perhaps the most surprising of all, but unlike against Holland this win edged a close contest rather than being against the run of play. When Iceland then completed the double over Holland (0-1) it looked like the move to 24 teams in the finals was really going to result in some really unlikely qualifications, and that Holland would miss out. Turkey spurned the chance to send the Netherlands into a remote 4th place (where not even a play-off could save them), by conceding a late, late home equaliser to Latvia, but by beating Holland in their next home game moved third. The Czechs won in Latvia and Iceland drew at home ensuring qualification for both, leaving the Dutch with an awful lot to do simply to get a play-off.

In the penultimate matches, Holland did win narrowly in Kazakhstan but Turkey beat the already qualified Czechs. This meant a home draw for Turkey in their last game would send Holland out; although that game for Turkey was v Iceland, the unlikely qualifiers had drawn their last two home games and now safely in France 2016 had ceased to look like world beaters. As it was, the Czechs topped the group after a Van Persie own goal allowed them to take a 0-3 lead in Holland; although by then reduced to 10 men they eventually held on to win 2-3, dumping out the Dutch, who wouldn't have qualified anyway because of Turkey's result. Turkey in fact beat Iceland with the latter proving that having no incentive is indeed a powerful disincentive as they went down 1-0 to finish second in the group.

In a bizarre twist, third placed Turkey also qualified automatically, heaping misery on a Greek population already dulled by austerity and their own team's failings. Kazakhstan's 0-1 win in Latvia, sent the Latvians (also qualifiers in 2004 when Greece won) bottom of the group. One third place team from all the groups was to qualify automatically on the basis of their record minus that of the last-place team (apart from group I, I assume, which had one team fewer). It was the Kazakhs' only win in qualifying. Turkey thus had their two draws against Latvia expunged (rather than their two wins against Kazakhstan) and progressed to France at the expense of....[3]

Group B

Picking up the pointless theme of what countries might be called, in European terms, Wales might easily be called 'Wails' having never qualified for the Euros, sometimes missing out very narrowly, but always missing out. So it made their start this time all the more remarkable, below Belgium at the halfway stage but with the same points and above (and beating) teams like Israel and Finland; hardly European giants, but historically more than a match for everyone's fave Principality.

Wales' win at home to Belgium was terrifying in a number of ways. First of all, the 1-0 victory over a team that the rankings touted as 'second best in the world'[4] was accompanied towards the end by a spine-tingling rendition of 'Land of my Fathers'. For those who have heard the scratchy rendition of the song by Cardiff fans in 1927 at Wembley before their infamous victory over the shiny-shirted gooners, it was *just* like that but without the scratchiness. Second, it resulted in an official warning from

---

[3] Read on!

[4] And who went on to be ranked number 1 in the world!

the publisher that casual rudeness to 'other' countries in the UK would no longer be tolerated because some of them might qualify and some of their population might now be potential customers to whom we should avoid rudeness. Fortunately though, he said nothing about the Republic, or France etc.[5] Qualification opened up further for Wales as Bosnia beat Israel with the help of Herzegovina. People remained cautious however, remembering famous football predictions like 'Smith must score'. Apart from anything else, Wales' win was based on a cool finish by the world's most expensive player and a huge rear-guard action (one third of both possession and shots); neither factor safe to rely on every week.

But one way or another, Wales went into their away match in Cyprus, both on the verge of qualification and also ahead of England in FIFA rankings for the first time (Wales at 9, England at 10). In a game short on action, Wales came tantalisingly close to European qualification with a single, late Bale goal; to Maradona's Argentina in 1990 and Le Tissier's Southampton in the mid-1990s we can now add Bale's Wales as the archetypal one man team[6] as he seems determined to single-handedly make them a force in World football. The usual managerial rhetoric is of a team which works hard, but Bale is the obvious plus factor for Wales. However, Bale failed to fire in the next game (a 0-0 home draw v Israel) and when Belgium then mimicked the Welsh result in Cyprus (late winner, only goal, world class player

---

[5] None of this is remotely true. Urbane are a splendid egalitarian publisher employing the finest authors and offering full artistic licence. And as for me, I'm called Lloyd and have played 4 different sports for Wales, so I'm hardly likely to be serious, am I? Boyo!

[6] *One Man Team* is also the name of my Le Tiss biography (2005) also available from Urbane

– this time Hazard) it meant Welsh qualification was still not assured even if a home game against Andorra from which 1 point would be required, actually looked a lot like 3 points.

It was a disconsolate Chris Coleman who then trudged from the field following Wales' subsequent 2-0 defeat in Bosnia or Herzegovina, until someone alerted him to Cyprus' win in Israel which meant Wales had qualified for a major tournament for the first time since 1958, nearly 60 years previously and for the Euros for the first time ever. They were weeping in the valleys (one imagines). Bosnia's win put them back in contention for a play-off place along with Herzegovina of course. Israel were not out of contention, although travelling to group leaders Belgium in their last game. Meanwhile Cyprus emerged from nowhere; by winning in Israel, they opened up the possibility of a play-off place if they could win at home to Bosnia. Err...quite remarkable, which is why I have remarked upon it here.

Briefly Wales were topping the group as they led Andorra before Belgium were doing likewise against Israel. But both teams won in the end to leave Belgium, now ranked by FIFA as the best team in the world (having failed to score against Wales in two matches?), top with Wales second.[7] The battle for a play-off spot was jolly exciting. Bosnia were in the box seat and just needed a win to secure the play-offs. They led in Cyprus early on, but conceded 2 quick goals. At that point Cyprus looked like they might pull off an extraordinary feat in a campaign of extraordinary feats; however, Bosnia went on to win 2-3 and hoped they might have a better campaign than during the World Cup if they

---

[7] 7 cleans sheets and 7 goals for Bale

could overcome the Republic of Ireland in the play-offs (which kinda gives some of the later story away but never mind!).

Group C

Spain, Euro Winners in 2008 and 2012 and World Cup Winners in between, were brought down to earth in Brazil where they exited early doors. Although winning four of their first 5 qualifying matches, the loss was to Slovakia who won all 5. Given that Slovakia had only 27% of possession, and 5 shots their 2-1 win might be considered a little lucky but it ensures that the veneer of invincibility surrounding Spain has well and truly worn off. Nonetheless, heading into the final round of games Spain (21) did lead Slovakia (19) by 2 points, with the Ukraine the only other team in contention a further 3 points back.

After winning their first 5 games, Slovakia slumped alarmingly with a point from the next three. Crucially, though, the point came in a 0-0 draw at home to Ukraine, meaning that prior to the last game, Slovakia led Ukraine on head-to-head record, having won 0-1 in Kiev or Donetsk (but probably not the latter). Slovakia travelled to Luxembourg, whilst Ukraine hosted European champions Spain. Surely the Slovaks would limp across the line to join the once conjoined but more beery Czechs? They did limp across the line with an unconvincing 2-4 victory in Luxembourg, consigning Ukraine to the play-offs.

Group D

Gibraltar scored their first competitive goal (obviously against fellow minnows Scotland) and conceded their first two dozen in double quick time. I mean what is the point?! Now imagine instead the following:

Minnow Group A or South	Minnow Group B or North
Malta	Liechtenstein
San Marino	Luxembourg
Gibraltar	Faroe Islands
Andorra	Guernsey
Monaco	Isle of Man
Greece	Shetlands
Faro Airport Staff Veterans XI	Dewsbury

The names are not important, but this lot play each other home and away at the same time as the qualifiers, and actually win a few games. Winner A plays runner up B and vice versa to create a final to contest a trophy: we'll call it The Pettiford Trophy after the visionary Englishman who invented it. Both finalists are 'promoted' to the European qualifying proper next time around, with the two worst teams in qualification, I dunno perhaps Scotland and Macedonia, being relegated. Surely to chuffing God that has to be better than perpetually finishing bottom of a group and/or having absolutely no chance of qualifying and only rarely even scoring a goal?

But anyway, Poland sneaked into an early lead thanks to

a 2-0 home win against Germany. Germany's 'nil' included 29 shots which must be getting close to a record for 'nil'. So much for that clinical ruthless streak that's won them a whole 1 world cup in the last 1000 years. As the second half of qualifying got underway, Poland crushed Georgia in Warsaw,[8] whilst Germany did the same to Gibraltar in, err, Portugal (of course). Meanwhile, John O'Shea scored an own-goal to give Scotland, playing in their traditional white, pink and yellow kit, a draw in Dublin.

Scotland remained in touch with Poland and Germany at the top of the group. As a result, I did become ever so slightly paranoid about all the pre-gloating over Scottish non-qualification. So it was with some relief that I tuned in halfway through the Scots' trip to Georgia to find the home team a goal to the good. I also noticed that their flag looked like the English one but with four little English flags in each quadrant. Nice. As you would expect, for a place where you could legitimately sing 'You're only famous for Stalin', the home side defended with plenty of steel and an equaliser looked about as likely as an escape from a Siberian gulag. Lee Griffiths joined Steven Fletcher up front for the last twenty minutes, but despite his apparent mission to get the whole world pregnant,[9] the Celtic striker never looked like scoring on this occasion. Of course every silver-lining has a cloud, and it was the Republic of Ireland who seized upon Scotland's misfortune to go third (with a stroll against Gibraltar), with one of the two looking destined to go in the play-offs behind Germany and Poland. And after Scotland scrapped valiantly in losing 2-3 at home to the

---

[8] I mean, I'm guessing Warsaw. It could have been Katowice or anywhere, but do you care and do I have time to look it up? No and no.

[9] If interested, google it!

Germans and the Republic beat the steely Georgians 1-0, it looked very much like Scotland would miss out altogether. Cue the celebrations/violins. Mainly celebrations.

And so to the final round of matches. Scotland did not qualify, thus meaning that I do not need to edit out all the gratuitous suggestions that this was inevitable. They had me worried as they came from behind to lead Poland 2-1, but then conceded an equaliser with the last kick. Oh dear, how sad, never mind. Meanwhile The Republic of Ireland beat Germany 1-0 with a goal from (Southampton's) Shane Long, so that the final matches became about which out of Poland and the Republic would qualify automatically with Germany and which would go into a play-off. As it turned out the difference between automatic qualification and the play-offs turned out to be Robert Lewandowski[10] – his winner for the Poles put his team through to the finals just below Germany who struggled to beat Georgia 2-1 (it's probably a psychological 'Stalin' thing). A 2-2 draw would have been enough for the Republic of Ireland, but down to 10 men the equaliser just wouldn't come. Gibraltar scored twice in approximately 1000 minutes, including time added on. They conceded 56 goals, more than the whole of group I. They need a defensive rock. Or perhaps a pitch on their rock where they can practise.

Group E

E is for England and 'elsewhere', which is where you will find a more detailed account of yet another easy qualifying campaign giving rise to insane hopes that we might finally

---

[10] He also top scored in qualifying with 13.

score one more than everyone else. In the 2004 volume I annoyed several readers by pointing out that the Republic of Ireland had no 'world class' players – well they didn't, and I will never concede that Roy Keane was other than a very nasty thug (unless he personally demands that I do, in which case I'll cave in instantly). But this time, I have to concede that whilst England may (at last) have promise, they very much fall into the category of 'no world class players'[11] They have absolutely no chance; they couldn't win if they played in 6000 years' worth of tournaments.

Group F

The team I mockingly called 'Northern Ireland Nil' for so long, finally found a way to score and win. At the halfway stage they were only behind Romania, having lost away to them, but they had also won in Hungary and Greece. Kyle Lafferty is one reason; he provided a target man and chipped in with key goals. Unplayed in the English Premier League by Norwich, he seems unplayable by opposition defences across Europe. But equally important was Southampton's Steven Davis' tireless running in midfield; with Northern Ireland playing without the ball for much of the time (only 26% possession in winning 0-2 in Athens, for instance) his reading of the game and disruptive impact on the opposition were crucial. It was surely not a coincidence that he was missing for the Romanian defeat? Possibly the biggest shock of early qualifying were the Faroes; only -5 goal difference after 5 games (compare that with Gibraltar -26, or San Marino -17) and with a 0-1 win in Athens and just a 1-0 defeat to Romania away. Greece were bottom

---

[11] How many of Rooney's goals have come at major championships?

2016 The Qualifying Campaign

after 5 games; oh how the incredibly lucky have been exposed as the truly awful team they are!

To mock me further, 2004 winners Greece completed the unlikely lose double against the Faroes; had everyone in Greece bet on this possibility they would no longer have a debt to worry about. Well, providing of course they'd all bet online with German book-makers, simultaneously and no-one ever exposed it as fraudulent, but I was more making a point rather than expecting you to analyse it like a Professor of European Economics. I mean, chillax man. Meanwhile Northern Ireland nil isn't such an insult when it's a creditable score against table topping Romania (also nil). The possibility of 4 home nations in a tournament remained very much alive, even though Scotland is one of them, so probably not.[12] Things could have been even better for NINIL™ but for a late Hungarian winner in Finland which kept Romania, NINIL and Hungary separated by a mere 3 points.

Romania and Hungary then drew whilst NINIL once again failed to live up to their now redundant nickname with a 1-3 victory against a spirited Faroe Islands team. In the next round of matches, the group looked to be about to become very tight; Romania drew again with Greece (0-0 obviously) whilst NINIL were losing 0-1 to Hungary and playing with 10 men. But in the 93rd minute, up popped Lafferty (again) to make NINIL qualification very likely, if not actually guaranteed. But like the Welsh, the month-long wait must have seemed agonising.

However, with Greece as the opposition, nerves were calmed early with a first half tap-in from (Southampton's,

---

[12] Honestly, these insults/accuracies were all in here way before Scotland fitted the description

did I mention that) Steven Davis. 30 years of hurt never stopped them dreaming as they demolished Greece 3-1 with a debut goal for the suspended Lafferty's replacement Magennis and a 15-yard header (yes, really) from Davis, who notched his third goal in a week (having scored for Southampton in a 1-3 victory over the champions at Stamford Bridge). Finland almost sneaked into contention with a win in Romania, but a last gasp equaliser meant that automatic qualification (along with NINIL) would go to either the unbeaten Romanians or Hungary, who fought back from a goal-down to win at home to the Faroes. So, in the final round Romania would be away to the Faroes and Hungary to Greece, with Romania just needing to match whatever Hungary did. It seems almost literally unbelievable that Hungary's task was easier on current form playing away to the 2004 winners, than Romania's.

Romania won 0-3 in the Faroes, making Hungary's defeat in Greece (4-3) irrelevant. Romania qualified below Northern Ireland, who topped the group with a 1-1 draw in Helsinki (probably). Greece, my tormentors of 2004, finished bottom of the group below the Faroe Islands on the basis of their head-to head-record. Hungary went into the play-offs with little confidence after losing in Athens (probably – I mean they definitely lost, it's just it could have been another city). Hungary's defeat to Greece was irrelevant in the sense also that Greece were pre-determined to finish in last place so that in calculating the one third-placed qualifier, results against Greece would be removed. This left the Hungarians assuming qualification until Kazakhstan's winner in Riga v Latvia (usual joke) allowed Turkey to sneak the qualifying spot reserved for the best third placed team.

And if we think 50 years since winning anything is a tough gig, spare a thought for the poor old Hungarians. Lost in the final in 1954 in an event so unlikely that even the confident Germans call it 'the miracle of Bern', and now with nothing more than memories and very occasional tournaments and a society blighted by post-communist rightist extremism. They did beat El Salvador 10-0 in 1982. Let us wish them well in the play-offs...although you'll see from my predictions below that I was not hopeful.

Group G

Liechtenstein won away to Moldova. They don't win often so I thought that was worth a mention. Their national anthem (Liechtenstein's that is) is sung to the same tune as 'God Save the Queen' which apparently led to an hilarious series of faux pas (fausse pas?) when the Republic of Ireland played there a number of years ago and wrongly assumed the British/English national anthem was being played in error and in place of their own. How very silly of them not to wait until lusty choruses of 'Up above the young Rhine' cleared things up for everyone.

7 wins out of their first 8 matches ensured that Austria were unlikely-ish runaway leaders, qualifying early and ahead of Russia (who, unlike England, sacked Fabio Capello just in time), Sweden and Montenegro. By the final matches, Russia needed just a point at home to Montenegro to consign Sweden to a play-off. Russia and Sweden both won, as did Austria who finished with 9 consecutive wins. Sweden to the play-offs, intriguingly against neighbours Denmark.

Group H

Croatia and Italy both found themselves undefeated at halfway, having drawn with each other. Croatia and Italy drew again in the second half of matches, this time behind closed doors. With both countries having something of a reputation for fascistic support (sorry, leftie Livorno[13] fans, but it's true) it was no surprise (OK, I guess it was) when carefully applied weed-killer allowed a swastika to appear on the pitch during the game. Croatia missed a penalty; Italy equalised with one.

As Italy trounced Malta 1-0 in game 7 (Southampton's Graziano Pelle saving Italian blushes), Croatia could only draw away to Azerbaijan. This meant that Norway's 0-1 victory in Bulgaria (secured by another former Saint, Forren) saw the top three teams separated by just 2 points, with Norway sneaking up on the rails, according to distinguished environmentalist Eivind Hovden due to a combination of 'a return to Drillo-style and big beards'.[14] Entering the final two games Italy led; 11 goals in 8 games including two 1-0 wins v Malta may not be very exciting, but was certainly effective.

Italy came from behind to beat Norway and qualified as group winners; since 6 of Norway's 19 points came against bottom placed Malta, their third place failed to win them automatic qualification. They were overtaken on the line by Croatia who held on to a 0-1 win in Malta. Bulgaria won at home in their last match; their first home Euro

---

[13] Apparently they celebrate Stalin's birthday; now that really is hardcore and blinkered!

[14] Harking back to Drillo Olsen's world boring/beating team of the 1990s, and even further back to rampaging Vikings.

qualifying win for a mere 8 years! Norway got Hungary in the play-offs in a tie that pundits are already describing as likely to lead to two international football matches being completed.

Group I

Smaller than the other groups, although this could have been resolved by throwing the Isle of Man or the Principality of Sealand in.[15] Most notable for Albania winning in Portugal early on in proceedings and then the "abandoned due to Albanian nationalist drone flying over the pitch leading to much fighting" match between Serbia and Albania. Serbia were docked points. By the time Portugal reversed their defeat to Albania (1-0 in Tirana)[16] the group had become a 3-horse race with Portugal favourites, followed by Denmark and Albania who were nip and tuck after a 0-0 draw in...well let's just say Copenhagen shall we, although could easily have been Herning, home of the mighty Midtjylland! All eyes moved to the Albania v Serbia fixture as potentially explosive and crucial.

Albania lost the grudge match, but with Denmark also losing in Portugal, Albania had the chance of an unlikely qualification if they could beat the group whipping boys Armenia. Albania (whose Football Association fails even to pre-date the first World Cup) did in fact beat group whipping boys Armenia 0-3 and so qualified for their first ever major tournament. Denmark moved to the play-offs, but since they won the whole tournament having been

---

[15] For the story of Sealand go here: http://www.sealandgov.org/ A crazy and interesting story

[16] Ditto the 'Warsaw disclaimer' above

eliminated prior to 1992, these probably hold no fear. If they lose they can   just wait for a political crisis to engulf someone before stepping off the beach to win again.

Full Time

This is what it all looked like when all ten of the group games were played:

Key:
Q = qualified
P = playoff
E = didn't qualify but exceeded expectations
D = donkeys

Qualifying Group A

Team	Won	Drew	Lost	For	Against	Points
Czech Republic **Q**	7	1	2	19	14	22
Iceland **Q**	6	2	2	17	6	20
Turkey **Q**	5	3	2	14	9	18
Netherlands **D**	4	1	5	17	14	13
Kazakhstan	1	2	7	7	18	5
Latvia	0	5	5	6	19	5

Qualifying Group B

Team	Won	Drew	Lost	For	Against	Points
Belgium Q	7	2	1	24	5	22
Wales Q	6	3	1	11	4	21
Bosnia & Herzegovina P	5	2	3	17	12	17
Israel	4	1	5	16	14	13
Cyprus E	4	0	6	16	17	12
Andorra D	0	0	10	4	36	0

Qualifying Group C

Team	Won	Drew	Lost	For	Against	Points
Spain Q	9	0	1	23	3	27
Slovakia Q	7	1	2	17	8	22
Ukraine P	6	1	3	14	4	19
Belarus	3	2	5	8	14	11
Luxembourg E	1	1	8	6	27	4
Macedonia	1	1	8	6	18	4

Qualifying Group D

Team	Won	Drew	Lost	For	Against	Points
Germany Q	7	1	2	24	9	22
Poland Q	6	3	1	33	10	21
R. Ireland P	5	3	2	19	7	18
Scotland D	4	3	3	22	12	15
Georgia	3	0	7	10	16	9
Gibraltar D	0	0	10	2	56	0

Qualifying Group E

Team	Won	Drew	Lost	For	Against	Points
England Q	10	0	0	31	3	30
Switz Q	7	0	3	24	8	21
Slovenia P	5	1	4	18	11	16
Estonia	3	1	6	4	9	10
Lithuania	3	1	6	7	18	10
San Marino D	0	1	9	1	36	1

Qualifying Group F

Team	Won	Drew	Lost	For	Against	Points
Northern Ireland Q	6	3	1	16	8	21
Romania Q	5	5	0	11	2	20
Hungary P	4	4	2	11	9	16
Finland	3	3	4	9	10	12
Faroe Islands E	2	0	8	6	17	6
Greece D	1	3	6	7	14	6

Qualifying Group G

Team	Won	Drew	Lost	For	Against	Points
Austria Q	9	1	0	22	5	28
Russia Q	6	2	2	21	5	20
Sweden P	5	3	2	15	9	18
Montenegro	3	2	5	10	13	11
Liechtenstein E	1	2	7	2	26	5
Moldova D	0	2	8	4	16	2

Qualifying Group H

Team	Won	Drew	Lost	For	Against	Points
Italy Q	7	3	0	16	7	24
Croatia Q	6	2	2	20	5	20
Norway P	6	1	3	13	10	19
Bulgaria	3	2	5	9	12	11
Azerbaijan	1	3	6	7	18	6
Malta	0	2	8	3	16	2

Qualifying Group I

Team	Won	Drew	Lost	For	Against	Points
Portugal Q	7	0	1	11	5	21
Albania Q	4	2	2	10	5	14
Denmark P	3	3	2	8	5	12
Serbia	2	1	5	8	13	4
Armenia	0	2	6	5	14	2

Serbia were deducted 3 points for getting a little bit fighty at home to Albania.

Extra time: The play-offs

The play-offs were played in mid-November 2015 (12th to 17th), so there was a month after the qualifying campaign to wonder and ponder and make predictions, so that is what I have done. See below. This will prove:

Either – I am a fantastic soothsayer and you should treat every other word in this book with extreme reverence, especially with a betting app in hand.

Or – I know about as much as you and Mark Lawrenson do and for reasons of historical accident find myself writing my twaddle out for people to read. Even so I will be as reliable as any expert you see on the TV.

[Odds at time of writing 1/7 on: 'Or']

Predictions (with seeded teams in bold)

Matches over 2 legs. Date played in brackets.

Norway v **Hungary** (12/11/15) 1-0

Hungary v Norway (15/11/15) 0-0

Norway to qualify (1-0 on aggregate)

Bosnia and Herzegovina v Republic of Ireland (13/11/15) 1-1

Republic of Ireland v **Bosnia and Herzegovina** (16/11/15) 0-1

Bosnia and Herzegovina to qualify (2-1 on aggregate)

Ukraine v Slovenia (14/11/15) 2-0

Slovenia v **Ukraine** (17/11/15) 0-1

Ukraine to qualify (3-0 on aggregate)

Sweden v Denmark (14/11/15) 1-1

Denmark v **Sweden** (17/11/15) 2-1

Denmark to qualify (3-2 on aggregate)

Actual Results (Prediction in brackets)

Norway v Hungary (12/11/15) 0-1 (1-0)

Hungary v Norway (15/11/15) 2-1 (0-0)

Hungary qualified (3-1 on aggregate)

Bosnia and Herzegovina v Republic of Ireland (13/11/15) 1-1 (1-1)

Republic of Ireland v Bosnia and Herzegovina (16/11/15) 2-0 (0-1)

Republic of Ireland qualified (3-1 on aggregate)

Ukraine v Slovenia (14/11/15) 2-0 (2-0)

Slovenia v Ukraine (17/11/15) 1-1 (0-1)

Ukraine qualified (3-1 on aggregate)

Sweden v Denmark (14/11/15) 2-1 (1-1)

Denmark v Sweden (17/11/15) 2-2 (2-1)

Sweden qualified (4-3 on aggregate)

Analysis of predictions

Hungary did qualify rather than Norway, so there's not much spinning that, except to say Norway dominated possession and had more shots in both games.

In the next tie, I accurately predicted the outcome of the first tie, spooking my co-author into requesting that I change my prediction for the second leg. Alas I was unable to do this, but he needn't have worried. My thinking in this prediction was that neither team was spectacular in attack and would get edgy at home, so that Bosnia would nick it in the away leg (presumably with an assist for Herzegovina). But it shows what a mug's game football betting is; really not a bad prediction at all, but you can't legislate for dodgy penalties and just as the Republic of Ireland failed to qualify for World Cup 2010 due to a handball which wasn't spotted, this time they went through with a not handball which was spotted (if you see what I mean).

Slovenia had previously won a play-off against Ukraine, but on this occasion (and entirely/exactly as predicted) lost the first leg in Kiev 2-0. They held a 1-0 lead in the home leg, but a late equaliser saw them off, once again 3-1 on aggregate.

Sweden looked home and dry at 2-0 up against neighbours Denmark. However, a late Danish strike gave them a precious away goal and everything to play for in the second leg. Alas, whilst Denmark scored the 3 goals when I predicted, Sweden managed an extra 2. Darn that Ibrahimovic!

Overall only one of the teams I predicted got through (Ukraine) so that looks pretty poor. On the other hand, two results spot on would have been enough to make a tidy profit at the bookies if the same sum had been put on the eight separate matches.

Anyway, with the qualifying teams now established, we can bring you the following…

List of teams who will participate in the finals (Euro 2016)

(Ranked by estimated annual consumption of beer per capita – it's a totally random, and largely accurate, **exclusive**)

Country	Estimated annual consumption of beer per capita (a recent year, probably 2012) in litres	Deaths per Hundred Thousand in Road Traffic Accidents (just to test a theory)
Czech Republic	148.6	6.54
Austria	107.8	5.17
Germany	106.1	3.94
Poland	98.5	10.42
Republic of Ireland	98.3	3.91
Croatia	85.9	9.47
Romania	83.2	9.39
Russia	74.1	16.42

Country	Estimated annual consumption of beer per capita (a recent year, probably 2012) in litres	Deaths per Hundred Thousand in Road Traffic Accidents (just to test a theory)
Belgium	74	7.37
Hungary	71.3	6.17
Slovakia	70.3	7.58
England	68.5	2.97
Northern Ireland	68.5	2.97
Wales	68.5	2.97
Spain	68.4	3.65
Denmark	62.1	3.96
Ukraine	61.6	10.04
Switzerland	58.3	3.61
Portugal	58	8.57
Sweden	52.9	2.36
France	48	5.65
Iceland	45	3.54
Albania	40	12.44
Italy	29	6.03
Turkey	13	12.23

The above table was exhaustively researched using Wikipedia with the following assumptions made:

Denmark failed to qualify, of course, but it only takes a civil war somewhere and they'll be back in, so I included them in the table.

Albania was calculated in my head according to World Health Stats on alcohol consumption overall and some random extrapolations which may not take account of back-yard stills.

France ditto and allowing for a strong bias in terms of wine, as opposed to beer, consumption.

Portugal, taken to be a bit lower than Spain due to a preference for wine/port.

UK: it looked like it might take some genuine research to differentiate between the three qualifiers, so I opted to give them all the UK figure. Probably since Scotland is also included in these figures the actual figures are lower. They drink a bit; just sayin' is all! This in no sense endorses a break-up of the different associations and the playing of a single Great Britain and NINIL team in future.

Anyway, assuming our readership is largely English, here's how we got there… sort of…

Eng-er-land's qualifying campaign[17]

I've never been a football hooligan. Too cowardly when sober. Too giggly when drunk. None of the fearsome hooligan 'firms' of the 1970s and 1980s had too many

---

[17] This section seeks to set a world record for gratuitous mentions of cherished sporting triumphs against Scotland

gigglers. Apart from the infamous Grimsby Gigglers, of course, whose firm fell into a giant bowl of Oxo and became a laughing stock. But even so, I have to admit that at times the heady cocktail of beer and nationalism has left me reflecting afterwards that I can be a complete cock when I put my lack of a mind to it. Nationalism, it seems to me, is the problem, since internationalism and beer simply leads to St Pauli-like choruses of 'Hoch die internationale Solidarität!' and hugging random Germans. Well for me at least. So remember, before you read my tongue in cheek jingoism below, we're just a pissy little island (or rather 'parts' of pissy little islands) with no more or less right to be proud of our country than anyone else. So when an obnoxious German or Spaniard tries to rub your nose in it, just turn the other cheek because ultimately as we know, God is an Englishman. (Yeah, I know, and I write this stuff sober!). So down to the qualification story which starts with a little song...

"He stands just over 6 foot 3, Rickie Rickie,[18]

He'll take us to the Premier League, Rickie Rickie,

He gets the ball, he takes the piss, he wears the shirt of Matt Le Tiss,

Rickie Lambert, Southampton's goal machine"

So sang Saints fans in League One (I first remember doing so myself in Hartlepool on a tropical November evening in fact).[19] And so he did, taking in the Johnstone's Paint Trophy on the way, leading to the equally memorable song

---

[18] Allegedly only 6 foot 2, but it doesn't rhyme

[19] When I say 'in fact' it could have been March or October but it was cool and damp.

sung to Chelsea and Man City: "Johnstone's Paint Trophy, you'll never win that!" Why do I mention this apart from gratuitously reliving the good times? The reasons are two. First is the remarkable resurgence of Southampton FC, although this is really gratuitously reliving the good times, and the reflection of that in the England team. When Wayne Bridge won an England cap in 2001, I bought a 'Bridge, 14' England shirt, and thought I would similarly honour all future Saints recipients. And so I next did with 'Lambert, 20' in 2013. Except I fell on hard times and Lallana, Rodriguez, Clyne,[20] Forster, Shaw and Bertrand made it seem pointless to own quite so many almost identical England shirts.

The other reason to mention the meteoric rise of Rickie is that his international career was both brief and exciting and extended into this qualifying campaign in a potentially critical way. Extraordinarily all Rickie's international, European and club ambitions almost came true (or came partially true) in a couple of short years when already into his 30s; Premier League football, playing for his home town Liverpool and scoring for them in the Champions League and, of course, a brief international career.[21] In international football, his debut involved coming off the bench at Wembley and scoring the winner against Scotland with his first touch – a characteristically powerful header. Having subsequently impressed with further goals and assists, he went to England's ill-fated efforts at Brazil's 2014 World Cup and got his dream move to Liverpool.

None of the above, save for his winner against Scotland

---

[20] I mean I knew he was better than Glen Johnson before the 2014 World Cup and Liverpool fans knew that too, so why didn't Woy given that he watched us every other week?

[21] Assuming Rickie's international days now to be over, he still won more caps than Matt Le Tiss!

(which I felt like mentioning again) was fairy tale stuff, but it was still an extraordinary story. Unlike Matt Le Tiss he blossomed late in his career – at a similar age Le God was well on the wane – but as a rags to riches story it's hard to beat. Tightening lids on beetroot jars one minute and training with Macclesfield and scoring the winner against Scotland the next. Yeah I know I mentioned that before, but no one Scottish will read this because they won't (didn't) qualify.[22] [23] Anyway, I suppose I ought to get around to England's qualifying campaign...

Much, I think, hinged on the first game, a tricky tie against Switzerland away. Although with hindsight qualification looks a formality, a loss in this opening away game would have put England on the back foot and who knows what may have happened from there. As it was, a decent away performance saw England enter the last minute with a slender 1 goal lead thanks to Danny Welbeck. With just 11 seconds of normal time remaining, off the bench came Rickie (see there was a point to all of that, beyond mentioning his winner against Scotland, because what I am about to convey might not have made sense without all that back story). So, to see out what turned into 6 minutes of injury time, England turned to Lambert to hold the ball up. And so he did, as well as cleverly retaining possession, taking a yellow card for the team and providing an assist for a nerve-calming second for Welbeck and England.

From that point onwards, England never looked back whilst Lambert's international career never really looked

---

[22] Spot held for gloaty or contrite footnote

[23] Gloaty not contrite footnote reads: Hate to say I told you so! Ha ha!

forwards. But this crucial cameo and scoring the winner against Scotland (which I may have mentioned before) are the stuff that most of us can only dream of, although I'd hasten to suggest that most, if not all, Englishmen and Englishwomen would be more than capable of scoring against Scotland. (Oh, I'm sorry, but let's face it, what are the chances of anyone not English bothering to read this chapter?)

[Publisher's Note: Frankly the authors are cheap, but I cannot allow them to go on and on and on like this without the right of reply. Accordingly, and spending some of the money I should have invested in decent writers in the first place, here is a riposte by Dougal T McGlashan – Patriot and Poet:

Aye right. The authors of this so-called book have fallen for the myth that Scotland actually wanted to qualify for this jamboree run by UEFA (Unmarked Envelopes For Advancement). But to anyone who actually studied the games and results, Scotland's plan was obvious. We have executed that plan perfectly, and it's what we always do. In short – be where England aren't (like: at the World Cups in 1974 & 1978). Whilst 'Mingland's' passage to these finals was not confirmed, Scotland went all-out for direct qualification. Then as the sassenachs got into a position where the play-offs were a possibility, God's Own Country eased off the gas. And once pure-hideous Albion[24] squeaked through the easiest group since Uruguay & Costa Rica's[25] in the 2014 World Cup finals, next summer got even brighter for relaxing Scottish fitba fans. The auld enemas

---

[24] Still preferring 'Perfidious' personally

[25] Very brave of a Scot to mention Costa Rica – Ed.

would all be out of the country for ten whole days, and they'd get pumped on the pitch. Allow me to put then...

The case against England: Or, you can shove they Euros up yer erse (sideways)[26]

Firstly, a deep philosophical question: Were the English always such pure bawbags?[27] Probably. Well that's that cleared up. But apparently it's no enough for a book. Let's use a favourite of the English media - the Second World War (yes younger readers: 'twas ever thus). To beat the Germans then, Churchill marshalled support from the Soviet Union. Two decades later, England returned to this method in buying their home World Cup, and as with tackling Hitler, simply needed to see one ball over the line. The referee's assistant (or rather, England's assistant) duly waved his red flag, and as the commentator said, it really was all over. All over the English media for the next 50 years.

Now the reality...In 1967, England's apparent world champion status was revealed for the sham we always knew. They came up against a typically more talented Scotland side, and an incorruptible set of officials, with the inevitable result. Thereafter, all footballing success in England has been driven entirely by Scots. The Leeds United team of the 70s – Scotland in white. Liverpool in

---

[26] For those of you bemused by 'Chewing the Fat', 'Mountain Goats' or Rab C Nesbit, here's more of the same bile-infused 'humour'!

[27] Google translate, anyone?

the 80s - Scottish. Even the Nottingham Forest and Aston Villa European Cup-winning sides were shot through with Irn-Bru. For the last twenty years, English football was so dominated by a Scot, that the EFA not only sought his advice on their choice of manager, they wanted him to be it. He did a perfect job (for Scotland) – continually refusing the EFA role, and instead recommending (un)successively: Eriksson, McClaren & Capello. And now – both the English national team, and their wealthiest club, are pinning their entire futures on a player who not only has the Scottish traits of being tiny, skilful and a bit chippy – but in being named after Stirling, he carries a proud history of Scottish resistance against land-grabbing southern despots (yes younger readers, trying to get on the housing ladder: 'twas ever thus). I hear the wee laddie only opted to play for England when he realised he wasn't good enough for Scotland. Must have been worse than the leaving of Liverpool.

To many Scots, the original English er, numpty,[28] was Jimmy Hill. Hill actually did many good things in football, chiefly ending the maximum wage. This would have endeared him to Scots, with our natural affinity for the working man against the oppressive (English) overlord. Further, as Scottish footballers were always more talented and valuable than the English, they benefited more from rising player salaries. Hill paid the price - the reactionary and morally questionable club owners of the day (yes younger readers learning French: plus ça change) saw

---

[28] Many a minute spent pondering before an acceptable word was chosen…

he was 'sent to Coventry (City)'.[29] Even then, the English moneymen were muttering about "It's our currency, we shouldn't be giving it to the Scots. They'll only squander everything on Darien Fletcher"[30]. However, any positive contribution from Hill was completely overshadowed (literally) by his chin, and (particularly) by his demeaning demeanour. Jimmy Hill may always have been a muppet, but like Kermit, this character really took hold once the English Broadcasting Corporation put him in front of a TV camera. Hill's provocative punditry peaked when he described the second-greatest goal in World Cup history as a 'toe-poke'. This twenty-yard screamer by David Narey for Scotland against Brazil (aye, that Brazil, the legends of 1982) was only bettered by Archie Gemmill's goal against 'total football' Holland.[31] Jealousy of nations with superior talent was always too evident with Hill, and he became simply a figure of fun. To be fair (as Scots are – we invented it), he took the retorts, along with everything else, on that chin.

Who will the Scots follow in Euro 2016? Well we won't adopt the English attitude and ignore it because we're not there. We'll watch the games on TV (invented by a Scot), whilst sitting on chairs (invented by a Scot), drinking beer (same) and breathing air (ditto). Rangers fans will follow follow Northern Ireland (and probably England),[32] Celtic fans will support the Republic of Ireland, whilst the actual Scotland fans on the civilised side of the Tweed will support

---

[29] A fate worse than a fate worse than death!

[30] Look up the 'Darien Scheme'

[31] They did fail to qualify on both occasions I think? - Ed

[32] Apparently there's a joke in that repetition for our Scottish reader!

any of the other teams. We just want football to be the winner – not England. Are we remotely concerned England might win it? Er, Naw. War, politics, football, refugees – England can't do anything in Europe without Scotland. We deliberately removed ourselves, to sit back and enjoy. Another failure awaits.

This summer under France's warm sun

Euro Twenty-Sixteen will be won

As for the English

Well they can but wish

That this time they get past round one

Dougal T. McGlashan[33] – Patriot and Poet]

Anyway, returning to the real world Dougal, although a formality, England still needed to build on the initial Swiss springboard to qualify. They did so with wins against San Marino 5-0 (Welbeck once again netting), Estonia 0-1 (with Lambert once again called upon to help protect a fragile lead) and Slovenia 3-1 (England finally conceding a goal, although scored by Jordan Henderson). Before beating Lithuania at home 4-0, Lambert made possibly his final appearance in an England shirt in a friendly thrashing of Scotland 1-3. At this stage five wins out of 5 at halfway suggested that England's tried and tested formula of 'easy qualification campaign, utter cock-up at the championship' was once again very much on the cards.

By the time England played Slovenia, Rickie had slipped

---

[33] The T stands for 'Tosh' obviously.

quietly from view as Wilshere scored 2 fantastic goals and Rooney the winner in a hard fought 2-3 victory. Glen Johnson was also fortunately discarded by this point – not being offered a contract by Liverpool, who also paid Southampton £12.5 million for Nathanial Clyne, told everyone who didn't already know, what Woy should have known *before* picking his Brazil squad (after all he was watching Southampton every week at that time).

Apart from Rooney who played as captain, Roy seemed to have the luxury in San Marino of fielding many fringe players such as Vardy and Shelvey. Rooney got the ball rolling with a penalty which brought him level with Sir Bobby Charlton as England's leading goal-scorer. England ran out 0-6 winners, including Walcott striking with his first touch off the bench and Kane finishing coolly in a way which pleasingly eludes him in a Tottenham shirt at the time of writing early in the 2015/16 season. Switzerland's qualification looked extremely unlikely as they trailed Slovenia at home 0-2 with about 10 minutes left on the clock; however they scored three times with a winner deep into injury time, allowing them to lose to England and still be clear in second.

Kane scored again in that home 2-0 win against Switzerland, but this round of matches will be remembered for a special moment and goal. Yes, San Marino scored in the group for the first time and very nearly left Lithuania with a point, denied only by a very late winner. Oh yes, and Rooney beat Bobby Charlton's record by netting for the 50th time in an England shirt. As ITV's commentary reminded us "that doesn't mean he's better than Bobby Charlton was" even if he may have found a better way to deal with baldness. England finished off with easy wins against Estonia (home) and Lithuania (away) to complete a 100% record at an average of more than 3 goals scored per game. Just 3 goals were conceded; one was a Jordan Henderson own goal and the other two were both away to play-off bound Slovenia. Switzerland finished second winning all but one of their non-England fixtures. So, an easy qualifying campaign... although we've been there before of course and sadly the most likely outcome is that Scotland will laugh longest in summer 2016.[34]

---

[34] Oh, and thanks for everything Rickie.

Qualifying Teams: Country by Country

Country / French Equivalent

France / La France
(but said like Inspector Clouseau would say it)

Road to qualification

Automatic as host nation. At the time of writing their form was good. The 2-0 defeat at Wembley to England will have been difficult in the context of terror attacks in Paris, but prior to that they had conceded only 2 goals in 4 consecutive wins which included clean sheets against Germany and Portugal.

Tournament history

World Cup: winners 1998; European Championship: winners 1984, 2000

Manager / Coach

Didier Deschamps (Desired One of the Fields). More than familiar to UK fans from his time as a player at Chelsea. For anyone that doesn't know him: depending on the direction of the wind, he's either a white-collar villain in *EastEnders* or a stunt-double for Bobby Davro.[1]

Players to watch

The mercurial Paul Pogba is an obvious choice, but there's still a part of us that thinks that if Karim Benzema turns up and scores to his potential (and bearing in mind the legal issues raging at the time of writing), he could have a real effect on the tournament. Any perceived shakiness in defence can be counteracted single-handedly by an in-form Hugo Lloris.

The word on the street

Our contact Christophe in Rouen reckons the French are quietly confident in their ability to bounce back from the disappointment of quarter-final exits in both Euro 2012 and World Cup 2014. Nantes remains unconvinced, however, as the interview earlier in the book suggests. The abomination of the November 13th 2015 terrorist attacks on Paris has, according to every French friend we've been

---

[1] Surely Bobby only does stunts in Spoonerismland

in touch with, instilled an even steelier sense of resolve in the players and the fans.[2]

Any good lookalikes?

Antoine Griezmann is versatile in this regard, being 'any USSR Olympic boxer circa 1980'. In Lookalikelandia, it's considered poor form to note that two international goalkeepers look like each other, but Hugo Lloris is unnervingly similar to Iker Casillas. Meanwhile on Broadway, Lucas Digne is defined as 'any actor playing the young Frankie Valli in *Jersey Boys*'. Finally, Raphaël Varane is what Patrick Kluivert and Jeremy Guscott behold when they look into their (shared) retrospective 'mirror, mirror on the wall'.[3]

Any good anagrams?

Loic Remy = Oily Merc.

Patrice Evra = Reactive Rap.

'Matuidi' ought to be (but isn't) an anagram of 'Cheryl's mother'.

Any songs I can sing if I fancy getting behind them?

Apart from perennial classics 'Joe le Taxi' by Vanessa Paradis and 'Chanson d'Amour' by Manhattan Transfer, there's a bunch of Paris-related titles, ranging from the

---

[2] Although how steely is, steelier than a vague disinterested shrug?

[3] Your other author is now feeling less guilty about the tosh he served up earlier

Style Council's topical 'Paris Match' and Blondie's 'St Denis Denis' to the late Gary Moore's phenomenal 'Parisienne Walkways'. Of most use, though, is the obligingly handy option of 'I Don't Speak French' by Girls Aloud.

Our prediction

Pilloried in the local press, rumours of fights in the dressing rooms, innuendo and insinuation haunting every training session, eventually ending in the semi-final.

Country /French Equivalent

Romania / La Roumanie

Road to qualification

Romania lost out to Northern Ireland by a single point at the top of Group F, remaining unbeaten with an impressive five wins and five draws, and conceding only two goals in the whole campaign, though with minnows Greece and the Faroes involved, it could have been a harder group for the Romanians. However, on the flip side, they scored only 11, and it is this that may sound alarm bells among the coaching staff as they look ahead to the finals.

Tournament history

World Cup: quarter-finals 1994; European Championship: quarter-finals 2000.

Manager / Coach

Anghel Iordănescu (Angel Son of Jordan). Iordănescu has successfully juggled careers in football (as a player and manager) and politics (he's a senator in his country's government). Currently in his third spell as national head coach, he benefits from a passing resemblance to most Soviet-era politicians from any country east of St Petersburg.

Players to watch

Recent squads have comprised players plying their trade in a wide scattering of countries across Europe and beyond, so we don't see many of them regularly, except maybe Gabriel Tamaş at Cardiff City, Costel Pantilimon at Sunderland and Florin Gardoş at Southampton (who will hope to be fit again). The undoubted star of the show, for us, is Gabriel Torje in midfield, with supporting cameos from Bogdan Stancu and Raul Rusescu up-front.

The word on the street

One of the assistants (Dan) in my local library is Romanian, and he told me all about the difficulty of recreating the consistency of the squad of the 1990s and early 2000s, when Hagi, Petrescu and Popescu were in their pomp. Dan agrees that firepower is a problem, and that his boys are unlikely to get out of the group, but thinks there's an outside chance if they can maintain their tight defence and scrape the odd goal on the counterattack.

Any good lookalikes?

Goalkeeper Ciprian Tătăruşanu keeps busy as an

uncredited understudy for Scottish-American entertainer John Barrowman, while his colleague Alexandru Măţel is chef James Martin. Constantin Budescu frequently has us rolling in the aisles/isles in his part-time role as Scottish comedian Kevin Bridges, while winger Ioan Hora recently distinguished himself by coming a creditable seventh in Romanian TV's smash hit Are You Xavi Hernández? Eth eth eth, peth eth eth, Chris Waddle.

Bonus Feature: DIY Joke

Stem: Name 3 Premiership footballers of the last 20 years who have been named after TV programmes.

DIY Bit: Gerry Taggart of Leicester City would be a good example, or Alexandre Songs of Praise.

Punchline: When the person is thinking hard for the third, you chip in with Dan Pet Rescue (erstwhile of Chelsea and Southampton)

Any good anagrams?

Andrei Ivan = Naive Drain.

Dan Nistor = Dr. Stain On.

Steliano Filip = I Oil Penis Flat.

Any songs I can sing if I fancy getting behind them?

Given Romania's chances at the Finals, we should perhaps begin with Extreme's 1992 ditty 'Bucharest in Peace'. Some excellent supportive work has been done in this context by Black Sea Sabbath, against the soundtrack of the Mock Turtles' 'Danube Dig It?' One little kiss isn't everything. (Would have been perfect if Filip Kiss was Romanian, but he's not)

Our prediction
Group stage exit

Country / French Equivalent

Albania / L'Albanie

Road to qualification

Albania nudged ahead of Denmark to finish in second place in Group I behind Portugal, thus achieving their first ever qualification for the finals of a major tournament. They did so partly with a tight defensive record, and partly via the outcome of DroneGate against the Serbian team in Belgrade. Fair play to them.

Tournament history

World Cup: never qualified; European Championship: debuting in 2016.

Manager / Coach

Gianni De Biasi (God is Gracious of the Bow-legged Stammerers).[4] A jaunty, pensionable-age Alan Shearer persisting with his Ken Livingstone impersonation party-piece. After an undistinguished playing career, De Biasi has really hit the jackpot with the Albanian national team, copping an undreamt-of Honour of the Nation Order in Tirana as a reward for reaching the 2016 finals.

---

[4] You really couldn't make this up, though I suspect we are most of the time

Players to watch

Hamdi Salihi and Edmond Kapllani should, between them, net any goals going at the tournament, but our fear is that these won't be many. Lorik Cana should use his experience to steady the ship at the back, and Rey Manaj might just provide a couple of surprises up-front.

The word on the street

We don't know any Albanians, so I emailed a Greek mate of mine who works in a hotel in Corfu that employs an Albanian gardener (part-time Tuesdays and Thursday mornings). Using Italian as a lingua franca, the latter confirmed that he once saw Ansi Agolli in a bakery in Tirana, but that apart from that he has no interest in football. As such, we remain none the wiser. Mysterious Albanians; it was ever thus.

Any good lookalikes?

Orges Shehi is the result of what will happen when Hristo Stoichkov and Neil 'Razor' Ruddock finally get it on. Sabien Lilaj is Marc Almond two weeks into a particularly harrowing stint in rehab. Taulant Xhaka and Amir Abrashi are twins. Bekim Balaj is a young Rod 'the Plod' Corkhill from *Brookside*. When Alban Meha wears his beard, he's Matt di Angelo from *EastEnders*, but clean-shaven he veers more towards the lovechild of Andrei Kanchelskis and Dimitar Berbatov.

Any good anagrams?

Etrit Berisha = His better air.
Lorik Cana = A rain lock.

Herolind Shala = Land hails hero.

Alban Meha = Ah, banal me.

Rey Manaj = Mary Jane.

Any songs I can sing if I fancy getting behind them?

Does anyone remember Tripping Daisy's 1996 hit 'Tirana'? No? Well, it only made Number 72[5] and graced the chart for a solitary week. On the other hand, 'Fier Comes the Summer' by the Undertones was a genuine smash. The problem here is that I don't know the names of many Albanian cities, so I'm stopping at two. You can have the Robert Palmer / UB40 duet 'Albania Baby Tonight', though.

Our prediction

Group stage exit

Country / French Equivalent

Switzerland / La Suisse

Road to qualification

The Swiss waltzed to second place in Group E behind England, and didn't perform badly. They're one of our cheeky bets for stealthy progress to the quarter-finals after a decent World Cup.

---

[5] The same position as the Undertones' 'Get Over You'. Just saying.

Tournament history

World Cup: quarter-finals 1934, 1938, 1954; European Championship: group stage 1996, 2004, 2008.

Manager / Coach

Vladimir Petković (Regal Son of Friday). Widely experienced as both a football manager and a Bosnian Father Ted.

Players to watch

England-based midfielders Gökhan Inler, Valon Behrami and Xherdan Skaqiri could put their experience to good use, and all are capable of chipping in goals. Leading the attack, Eran Derdiyok is the main man to turn games with his aerial power and all-round strength.

The word on the street

Several friends-of-friends from Winterthur and Bern provided analysis for us, and the common denominator was that the Swiss are well placed to eclipse their previous European Championship performances and replicate something of the stylish play and fighting spirit that took the nation to World Cup respectability back in the days of baggy shorts (first time round).

Any good lookalikes?

There's definitely a hint of both Wayne Rooney and Kevin Kilbane in Stephan Lichtsteiner – you decide. Michael Lang is Mackenzie Crook playing Kurt Cobain in a Nirvana biopic. Xherdan Skaqiri is a young Harry Enfield trying out an early impersonation of a young Graham Norton. You couldn't make it up – oh sorry, we did.

Any good anagrams?

Roman Bürki = Rum Knob Air.

Fabian Frei = A naïf fibre.

Renato Steffen = Nearest off net.

Any songs I can sing if I fancy getting behind them?

Leaving aside Del Shannon's timeless 'Swiss Maid', we have a wealth of crap punnery available to us here. If you're not familiar with the work of Zurich Astley, you could go straight for Ash's 'Berne Baby Berne', Chicago's 'If Geneva Now', Toni Basel's back catalogue, the Police's 'Lausanne', various artists' attempts at 'Walking in a Winterthur Wonderland', and a rousing singalong of the Kenny Rogers classic 'You Picked a Fine Time to Leave Me, Lucerne'.

Our prediction

Quarter-finals

GROUP B

Country / French Equivalent

England / L'Angleterre

Road to qualification

Dealt with in detail elsewhere in the book, but for now, suffice it to say that England's campaign was as near as damn it perfect. What that implies for the tournament itself is anyone's guess – or at least Lloyd Pettiford's.

Tournament history

World Cup: winners 1966; European Championship: 3rd place 1968, semi-finals 1996

Manager / Coach

Roy Hodgson (King Son of Hodge). A wise, multilingual owl, far too decent a man to be at the cut-and-thrust of international football management. Justice would be done if the lads could bring him some success in France.

Players to watch

Hodgson has brought in a wide range of youngsters with confidence and pace as their common denominator. The likes of Kane and Vardy ought to be able to shine, but most eyes will be on Wayne Rooney to perform on the big international stage the way he has at every other level. Let's also put forward Lallana, Alli and Dier as tournament high-achievers in the making.

The word on the street

None needed. All readers will have their opinions. The common thread is that England are capable of great things, but will they keep their bottle against the strongest European opposition?

Any good lookalikes?

Eric Dier is most of the Icelandic midfield, while John Stones is the improbable lovechild of Gary Lineker and that bloke George from Union J. Harry Kane's lookalike is very specific: 'a considerably shorter Peter Crouch playing a slick-haired dandy in any Charleston-themed musical soirée'.

Any good anagrams?

Harry Kane = Rare Hanky.

Jesse Lingard = Jingle Red Ass.

Eric Dier = Ice Rider.

Adam Lallana = Mad, Anal La La.

Any songs I can sing if I fancy getting behind them?

Anyone looking for inspiration beyond the usual 'Land of Hope and Glory', 'Three Lions' and 'Vindaloo' could consider the Angelic Upstarts anthem 'England'. Just a thought.

Our prediction

Semi-finals, many tears and another terrible refereeing decision

Country / French Equivalent

Russia / La Russie

Road to qualification

Finishing second behind runaway winners Austria in Group G, Russia performed solidly without distinguishing themselves, doing just enough to keep Sweden in third place. Notable was their defensive record: only five conceded in ten games, the same as Austria.

Tournament history

World Cup: 4th place 1966 (no, no, that was the USSR); European Championship: winners 1960.

Manager / Coach

Leonid Slutsky (Lion-like Son of Prostitute). We'll let you do your own anagrams. Suffice it to say that, as Slutsky is not one of the better known managers on the European circuit, for orientation you should be thinking along the lines of any ill-advised online-dating boyfriend encountered by *Coronation Street* siren Eileen Grimshaw, as played on screen by a fat Tom Hanks. His managerial involvement has been limited to club and country within Russia, but the peak of his career is surely the incident that is alleged to have put paid to his playing days: he fell out of a tree while rescuing a cat and buggered his knee.

Players to watch

Aleksandr Kerzhakov is the country's leading scorer, but we think the limelight (and goal-scoring duties) could easily be rotated around Aleksandr Kokorin, Artyom Dzyuba and Fyodor Smolov, all of whom have enjoyed good recent form.

The word on the street

We didn't fancy our chances in getting the word on the Russian street in any literal sense, but managed to find an exchange student, who asked us to refer to him only as "Alex". This we were happy to respect. He said that Shirokov can always be relied upon, but that he and his friends back home have no faith in the frontline if Kerzhakov has an off-day.

Any good lookalikes?

Any official lookalikes probably have to be sanctioned by the Kremlin, so the following suggestions are officially unofficial. If you look at Vladislav Ignatyev from far enough away, he's actually Nicky Butt. Viktor Vasin was expelled from John O'Shea's extended family at an early age for having 'too angry a look on him'. Meanwhile, in the burgeoning world of one goalkeeper looking like another, Igor Akinfeev has been fulfilling a useful role recently standing in for Steve Harper when the latter fancies a day off in downtown Hull.

Any good anagrams?

Aleksei Ionov = As One Evil Oik.

Igor Portnyagin = Gay Ring Portion

Oleg Ivanov = Go Love Ivan

Oleg Shatov = Love to Shag

Any songs I can sing if I fancy getting behind them?

Against a lilting backdrop of Sting's 'Russians' or Lisa Stansfield's 'So-Ve-It', we dig further into the cultural possibilities of this enigmatic country, and come up with work by Jennifer Rushian and Patrice Rushen. Symbolically, though, we are driven to rueful ecstasy by Doctor Feelgood's 'Putin Out of your Mind'. Putin on the Ritz by whoever the hell that was by.

Our prediction

Last 16

Country / French Equivalent

Wales / Le Pays de Galles

Road to qualification

Wales astonished a lot of people by bossing Group B for much of the campaign, being pipped by Belgium in the final run-in. As much as individual skill, this speaks volumes about a) how well Chris Coleman has marshalled his troops

Qualifying Teams Country by Country

and fostered a never-say-die spirit in the squad, or b) the individual skill of Gareth Bale.

Tournament history

World Cup: quarter-finals 1958 and we would have won it too, boyo, if it wasn't for that injury to John Charles – only just lost to Brazil, mind; European Championship: 2016 is debut year for Wales.

Manager / Coach

Chris Coleman (Bearer of Christ Charcoal Burner). A smooth but internally fiery character, who takes no shit and is resolute in his defence of his players and his country. Appearance-wise, he provides a ready-made solution to the eternal conundrum: what would Gareth Southgate look like after six weeks on a sunbed?

Players to watch

Bale aside, it will be interesting to see if Joes Ledley and Allen can perform at this level in midfield – form suggests they can. Up front, Simon Church's experience and hard work should really have produced more goals – maybe now will be his time? The biggest unknown, however, remains the fitness and impact of Aaron Ramsey.

The word on the street

The nation is awash with justifiably upbeat appraisals of how Wales are likely to fare. They handled Belgium pretty well in qualifying, so why shouldn't they mix it with the best Europe has to offer. I've heard talk of them reaching the semis, and of bottling it and going home after the group stage. On balance, and despite a huge desire to see the Welsh boys do well, our fear is that they might be stifled in midfield, that Bale will be man-marked throughout, and that they will underperform in the group. On the other hand, if Bale can do his wobbly, toddler tantrum inside the penalty area...

Any good lookalikes?

Sam Ricketts is Bradley Walsh, and David Vaughan is a cross between Level 42's Mark King and actor Toby Jones. Shaun MacDonald falls somewhere between Andrew Marr wearing a comedy ginger wig and Billy Mitchell from *EastEnders* (also wearing a comedy ginger wig).

Any good anagrams? (no, so surely you can do better?)

Sam Vokes = Ask Moves

Any songs I can sing if I fancy getting behind them?

If Saint-Etienne's 'Bale Movie' is a little low-key for you, you could try Miley Cyrus's 'Wrexham Ball', The Kinks' 'Cymru Dancing' or anything by the Cardigans. I was happy in the haze of a drunken hour but bread of heaven knows I'm miserable now...

Our prediction

Group stage exit

Country / French Equivalent

Slovakia / La Slovaquie

Road to qualification

Much to Europe's surprise, it was nip and tuck with Spain at the top of Group C for much of the qualifying campaign, before a relieved Spain pulled away, leaving a relieved Slovakia to limp over the qualifying line, a creditable second ahead of Ukraine.

Tournament history

Not much to shout about, though they did reach the Round of 16 at the 2010 World Cup. The glory days came before the dissolution of Czechoslovakia, when the combined team were World Cup runners-up in 1934 and 1962, and won the European Championship in 1976. Still reeling from the PR disaster of not insisting on Slovakoczechia with the capital in beautiful Bratislava.[6]

Manager / Coach

Ján Kozák (John Cossack). A latter-day Jan Molby with Donald Pleasance's eyes superimposed.

Players to watch

Captain Martin Škrtel can be trusted to hold a stiff line at the back, as well as popping up for a useful header now and then. We're looking to Róbert Vittek to provide most of the firepower up-front, but have a sneaky suspicion that

---

[6] Alliterative and inaccurate

Filip Hološko could have a lot to offer if Kozák gives him the nod.

The word on the street

Contacts in downtown Bratislava were a bit thin on the ground until we were put in contact with visiting student Hana, who knows her football. The Slovaks, she tells us, are realistic about their overall chances, but at the same time buoyed by performances in qualifying. Her private (now public) shout-outs as stars of the tournament are forwards Marek Bakoš and Adam Nemec.

Any good lookalikes?

Michal Ďuriš is a handy stunt double for a young Gary Numan.

Lukáš Tesák is reputed to be the lovechild of Nicky Butt and *Coronation Street's* Ashley Peacock.

Any good anagrams?

Ján Greguš = Anger Jugs

Martin Škrtel = Mr Latent Risk

Any songs I can sing if I fancy getting behind them?

OK, hold onto your hats here. First up is 'Slovak the River' by James Bay, followed by 'Slovak Hand' by the Pointer Sisters and 'Slovak My Bitch Up' by the Prodigy.

Our prediction

Group stage exit

GROUP C

Country / French Equivalent

Germany / L'Allemagne

Road to qualification

Unexpected hassle in Group D came in the form of Nonquallandia (in the earlier stages) and the Republic of Ireland (who pulled off one of the surprises of the group by beating the mighty Germans 1-0 in Dublin), but it was the head-to-head at the top with Poland that provided the sternest test, the Germans edging it in the end by a single point.

Tournament history

World Cup: winners 2014, only 2014; European Championship: winners, 1996.

(We should grudgingly note that *West* Germany did win the world cup in 1954, 1974 and 1990 and the Euros in 1972, 1980. However East Germany also entered these tournaments and that's cheating. Plain as.)

Manager / Coach

Joachim Löw (Joachim Lion). Highly successful international Manager / Coach. Best to look beyond his famed nose-picking and resultant-snot-munching antics, and focus instead on how Chachi from *Happy Days* is handling life at the helm of the German side.

Players to watch

It's time for Toni Kroos to step forward and blow the continent's socks off with his high-quality passing and shooting. If we leave goal machine Thomas Müller out of the equation, there's got to be a good chance that Max Kruse and Mario Götze will shine up-front.

The word on the street

German fans are understandably confident ahead of the tournament, but with a hint of caution. Our contact Michael in Düsseldorf eagerly awaits a string of fluent performances to match Germany's demolition of Brazil at the World Cup in 2014, and who would bet against that happening? It should be close at the top end, and Michael nods glumly in agreeing that Spain have got to be in with a serious chance of pipping Germany to the post.

Any good lookalikes?

André Schürrle is defined as 'either of the two members of A-ha who aren't Morten Harket'.

Any good anagrams?

Toni Kroos = Oink Roost
Erik Durm = Dire Murk

Any songs I can sing if I fancy getting behind them?

Of course. Kraftwerk's 'Autobahn' is the classic way to kick off if you take a wrong turn at Dover. 'Drowning in Berlin' by The Mobiles is still fondly remembered by legions of fans who either lived through the 1980s or saw their national side being hammered by the Germans in the capital. 'German Free Adolescence' by X-Ray Spex could be the tune of choice for those of a punkier persuasion, while punning rock fans will be amply catered for by anything by Bonn Jovi. You could do worse than 'Get Down On It' by Kool and the Baader-Meinhof Gang – but not much worse, admittedly!

Our prediction

Runners-up and at least they do play decent football these days, unlike the dire passing across the back four in the days when passing back to the keeper was an option.

Country / French Equivalent

Ukraine / L'Ukraine
(think Clouseau again)

Road to qualification

Slovenia were widely reported to have been 'spirited' in the play-offs. Whether this meant they were tanked up with vodka we don't know, but over the two legs, the Ukrainians were too strong for them, thus gaining revenge for a previous world cup exit.

Tournament history

World Cup: quarter-finals 2006; European Championship: group stage 2012.

Manager / Coach

Mykhaylo Fomenko (Who is like God? Son of Thomas). Whilst Fomenko's coaching skills have never been in question, his media savviness is reputed to derive from six years as Len Reynolds in *Emmerdale* followed by two as next-door neighbour Joe Carroll in the *The Royle Family*.

Players to watch

Yevhen Seleznyov is the leading gun up-front in terms of recent form, but much of Ukraine's goal power has come from midfield, via the likes of Andriy Yarmolenko and Oleh Husyev. We have a feeling in our water that Yarmolenko might be the most effective Ukrainian, but that his efforts might come to nothing if the rest of the team freeze on the big occasion.

The word on the street

The Ukrainians we've contacted all made much of the inter-club rivalry in the national squad – roughly 80% of recent squads have come from just four clubs: Shakhtar Donetsk, Dynamo Kyiv, Dnipro Dnipropetrovsk and Zorya Luhansk. In each case, robust cases were made for the importance of local players, but this didn't really give us much sense of national togetherness. Strange that. Not. The Dynamo fans were perhaps the most vocal in bigging up the national team's chances, but none of them mentioned progress to the quarter-finals. Nor did we.

Any good lookalikes?

Ruslan Rotan is the grandson of cuddly icon Bill Turnbull from BBC *Breakfast*, and is joined in BBC showbizland by Denys Oliynyk, who is the Scottish nutter who abused his wife Little Mo on *EastEnders*. Also on the telly, goalkeeper Andriy Pyatov is chirpy gardener Monty Don, and Oleksandr Kucher is practically the entire male cast of *Shameless*.

Any good anagrams?

Artem Kravets = Starve Market.

Taras Stepanenko = A steak repast? Non!

Denys Boyko = Yes, Do Bonky!

Any songs I can sing if I fancy getting behind them?

We have to dip into cod phonetics here to indicate the cultural importance of Kim Wilde's 'You Crane'. Illustrating the breadth of talent available to us in the Ukraine is 'Odessa Kind of Hush (All Over the World)' by the Carpenters, and The Who's 'The Kievs are Alright'. Of more recent significance was the Pussycat Dolls' 'Donetsk You Wish Your Girlfriend Was Hot Like Me?', or Kylie Minogue's 'Kharkiv You out of my Head'. That's probably more than enough to be getting on with, but we could maybe top things off with 'Crimea River' before Russia nicked it.

Our prediction

Group stage exit

Country / French Equivalent

Poland / La Pologne

Road to qualification

The Poles must have looked smugly at the naked Group D 18 months ago and thought, right, that's us and Germany through, then, especially after their early doors victory against the Germans. So it proved, but not before some monumental pressure applied by fellow pesky Catholics the Republic of Ireland. In the end, a single point separated the Germans and the Poles at the top, which I'm sure the latter would have taken at the outset. They scored freely in their ten games, especially Lewandowski, although 15 of their 33 goals came against Gibraltar (who also scored against Poland, one of only two goals they managed in the entire campaign).

Tournament history

World Cup: 3rd place 1974, 1982; European Championship: group stage 2008, 2012

Manager / Coach

Adam Nawałka (Ground/Earth, err, Nawałka). Relatively little is known worldwide about the coach, and this includes me. However, he's done a good job in the qualifying campaign. If you're unsure what he looks like, think 'dashingly trendy cardinal with a cushy administrative job at the Vatican and a cheeky glint in his eye, who drives the nuns wild'.

Players to watch

As we all know, Robert Lewandowski has been on blistering form for both club and country. The quandary is who will accompany him in Euro 2016 (and replace him when he retires), and the answer seems to be Arkadiusz Milik, who at 22 is already into double figures in his national goal tally. Midfield goals are also likely to come from Grosicki, Mila and Błaszczykowski, and this should be enough to get the Poles out of their group. Beyond that – and despite their performance in qualifying – we just feel they'll come unstuck in the last 16.

The word on the street

Peter is a UK national with Polish parents; he's bilingual and devours the Polish sports press whenever he can. His verdict is that if Lewandowski is on fire, the team can reach the heights of the 1970s glory days of Grzegorz Lato et al; if not, he has concerns. What sort of concerns? 'Just concerns.'

Any good lookalikes?

The entry on France makes reference to Hugo Lloris looking like Iker Casillas, flying in the face of goalkeeping lookalike etiquette. However, we're on similarly shaky turf here, noting that Artur Boruc is more than capable of standing in for Shay Given if the latter is indisposed. It's a little known fact that Kamil Glik dropped out at the first qualifying round of the 'We want a blond Bond' competition, eventually won by Daniel Craig. For his freestyling audition, he had to meet the 'can you be both Kasper Schmeichel and Freddie Flintoff simultaneously?'

challenge, and whilst he strove valiantly, he couldn't quite nail the pie-eating sub-element.[7]

Any good anagrams?

Karol Linetty = No tart likely or On likely tart

Sebastian Mila = I'm a snail's beat.

Robert Lewandowski = I stand below worker.

Any songs I can sing if I fancy getting behind them?

Most of the 1970s glam rock hits by Marc Poland could be put to good use here, as could the work of Warsaw (an early version of Joy Division). It's been a long time since Ringo Starr's 'Kraków Boogaloo' enjoyed an outing in any context, so now could be the time. Or perhaps not. Much more hummable are Mud's 'The Katowice Crept In', Harry Enfield's 'Łódź-a-Money' and David Bowie's 'Let's Gdańsk'

Our prediction

Last 16

---

[7] Proving that both authors are fluent in 'bollocks'

Country / French Equivalent

Northern Ireland / L'Irlande du Nord

Road to qualification

The boys stunned much of the world by winning Group F by a single point over Romania. No play-offs, no early departure, no messing about. Many people (ourselves included) fancy them to get out of their group at the Finals.

Tournament history

World Cup: Quarter-finals 1958, 1982; European Championship: debuting in 2016.

Manager / Coach

Michael O'Neill (Godlike Son of Niall). O'Neill has undoubtedly worked wonders at the helm of the Northern Irish squad, and is rightly lauded by fans and players alike. Facially, he is best described as 'Teddy Sheringham after a couple of troublesome years in frontline politics'.

Players to watch

The experience of Steven Davis will surely be key as the North step up to their first Euro finals. Up-front, we can't help but look to the goals of Kyle Lafferty as the recipe for success. Beyond that, keep an eye on one or two of the Scottish-based forwards: perhaps Liam Boyce, Billy McKay or Josh Magennis (nice to see some involvement for Nonquallandia).

The word on the street

Fans I've spoken to in Belfast and Derry are understandably bullish. The only weak link seems to be where the goals will come from if Lafferty gets injured or has an off-day.

Any good lookalikes?

Oliver Norwood is former Westlife singer Brian McFadden with a soupçon of the early Gary Pallister. Josh Magennis is the original Ronaldo.

Any good anagrams?

Liam Boyce = Malice Boy
Chris Brunt = Burn Christ

Any songs I can sing if I fancy getting behind them?

The purist within me cries out to get the music of Stiff Little Fingers adopted formally in support of Northern Ireland for Euro 2016, but a more likely scenario is equally acceptable wall-to-wall coverage of the Undertones' greatest hits. From the charts of yesteryear, you've got various melodies under the titles of 'Belfast', 'Belfast Boy' and 'Belfast Child', but there are also options from Status Quo ('Down Down'), Tom Jones ('Armagh Told Me not to Come') and UB40 ('Fermanagh Rivers to Cross'). The back catalogue of They Might Be Giants Causeway could be worth a spin, too.

Our prediction

Last 16

GROUP D

Country / French Equivalent

Spain / L'Espagne

Road to qualification

After what was initially an epic battle with Slovakia at the top of Group C, *La Roja* came good to win the group fairly comfortably. Have they peaked after a flurry of recent tournament wins? We think 2016 could see the Spanish back to their best.

Tournament history

World Cup: winners 2010; European Championship: winners 1964, 2008, 2012

Manager / Coach

Vicente del Bosque (Vincent of the Woods). Cesc Fàbregas has said of him, "he is a bit right-wing, shall we say", and although he has not reached the racist depths of Luis Aragonés, his predecessor, he has appeared to trivialise the problem of racism in Spanish football. He has, furthermore, attempted to aggravate equality and diversity advocates everywhere with these comments attributed to him after Ireland's exit from Euro 2012: "There is a blind team in the village I grew up in. They are of all ages and completely blind. They play with a ball that has a little bell in it and they even have some women playing for them. They would have put up a better show than the Irish." He then went on to describe the Irish as "a nation of flare-wearing, pasty-skinned troublemakers." One Irish fan attributed this to jealousy because VDB looks like a bus conductor. Even my co-author has shied away from such provocation. As with Mourinho, he can perhaps get away with outrage because he has an excellent record in management at both club and national level. Much hilarity can be had by googling images of him as a player and thus understanding the inspiration for several of the characters in both the 'Channel 9' sketches on *The Fast Show* and the 1970s sitcom *Mind Your Language*. The evidence suggests that Professor Robert Winston may have played in the same XI (or perhaps been driver on the same bus).

Players to watch

There's quality throughout the squad, but this might be the moment for Alvaro Morata to shine on a bigger stage. Equally, Sergio Busquets has for a long time hidden under the shadow of more widely celebrated midfielders Xavi and Iniesta, so perhaps 2016 could give him room to breathe and bring him to more serious prominence.

The word on the street

Our contact Javi in Valladolid talks measuredly about the effect on the squad of the retirements of Xavi and David Villa. It will, he says, be a matter of confidence – hoping that everyone can play to their potential and not lose their nerve. Midfield control will, as in previous tournaments, be key.

Any good lookalikes?

Fertile ground in the Spanish ranks:

Defender Mikel San José remains pencilled in as a future replacement for the role of Martin Fowler in *EastEnders*.

Juanfran is a hardworking geography teacher in a Rotherham comprehensive school.

Run Santi Cazorla through that software that ages your face and note with glee how he turns into chef Gennaro Contaldo.

Isco is comedian Jack Whitehall.

David Silva is Duncan from Blue.

Any good anagrams? (And a bad one)

Nolito = Lotion

David Silva = Valid Davis

Any songs I can sing if I fancy getting behind them?

If you're fed up with the obvious 'Y Viva España' by Sylvia (who, needless to say, was Swedish), try a rousing rendition of Freddie Mercury and Montserrat Caballé's 'Barcelona' or Frank Sinatra's 'Granada'. Mink De Ville's 'Spanish Stroll' is well worth bearing in mind, too, unlike the Clash's 'English Seville War', which – although a great song – is also a shit pun.

Our prediction

They will pass the ball to death until it retreats into the goal from fright. Winners.

Country / French Equivalent

Czech Republic / La République Tchèque

Road to qualification

The Czechs pulled off a wholly unexpected feat by qualifying from Group A alongside the cheeky Icelandic upstarts, at the expense of tournament veterans Holland and many people's outside bet, Turkey. They did so with style, and fair play to them.

Tournament history

World Cup: first round 2006; European Championship: runners-up 1996. As is the case with Slovakia, the golden era was under the former Czechoslovakian flag.

Manager / Coach

Pavel Vrba (Paul Willow). Vrba has an impressive record of club management, being voted Czech coach of the year on five occasions, and has had a decent run at the helm of the national side so far. Appearance: the guy sitting behind Putin at Kremlin press conferences, smirking slightly because he knows something you don't.

Players to watch

There's an alarming shortage of international goals among many of the players called up over the last couple of years to represent the Czech Republic. It may be that there will be too much reliance on Arsenal's Tomáš Rosický – though we all know he can deliver. Keep an eye on another player with experience in the English system: Matěj Vydra.

The word on the street

Confidence is not lacking on the streets of Prague, from where Anna emailed to say that Vrba's attacking philosophy has made the Czechs fearless going forward, but that this might leave them vulnerable to being caught on the break. We should "expect a couple of 3-2 victories".

Any good lookalikes?

On a recent episode of the Czech version of genealogy series *Who Do You Think You Are?* it was revealed that, in the 1840s, distant relatives of Dennis Bergkamp and Boris Johnson had got jiggy at a party in downtown Prague, sowing the seed for the phenomenon that would later be known as David Limberský.

There is a rumour that Daniel Kolář was kidnapped and smuggled into the Czech camp following a midnight raid on the Iceland squad's hotel in 2015. To counter this rumour, his 'people' confirmed that he is set to play the lead role in the forthcoming biopic of Jordi Cruyff.

Any good anagrams?

Daniel Pudil = Lined Up Laid
Jan Kopic = Jock Pain

Euro 2016

Any songs I can sing if I fancy getting behind them?

LA Mix's 'Czech This Out' should serve to get the party started, before Queen's 'Bohemian Rhapsody' kicks in, topped off by Ellie Goulding's 'Brno'.

Our prediction

Quarter-finals

Country / French Equivalent

Turkey / La Turquie

Road to qualification

Turkey finished third behind the Czech Republic and Iceland in the weirdest, least predictable of the qualification groups. Their 18 points secured them automatic qualification as best-performing third-placed country, thanks to the unlikely result Latvia 0 Kazakhstan 1. It's all explained above and led to much weeping and gnashing of teeth in Budapest and Amsterdam.

Tournament history

World Cup: 3rd place in 2002; European Championship: semi-finals 2008.

Manager / Coach

Fatih Terim (Conqueror Term). Terim has built up a strong reputation as a no-nonsense coach during three spells at the national helm, as well as club-level stints in Turkey and Italy. He is a portmanteau of Sir Alan Sugar, Vicente del Bosque and Michael Barrymore – or Sir Vicente Barrymore, if you will. More importantly, he is an anagram of 'Hi-fat merit'.

Players to watch

Barcelona's Arda Turan leads an organised midfield that's not short of experience or goals. The main striking power is likely to come from Burak Yılmaz.

The word on the street

My mate Paul – who has lived in Turkey for a few years – draws our attention to the fact that the squad is reasonably settled, with the vast majority playing in the Turkish league and hence knowing each other's games inside-out. His assessment of the Turkish press is that the country is brimming with confidence.

Any good lookalikes?

Emre Çolak could pass for any cocky, trim-bearded sous chef fancying his chances on BBC *Masterchef*. Alper Potuk is a youthful Pep Guardiola partially disguised as Mr Claypole from *Rentaghost*. Mert Günok is 'Roman Abramovich 20 years ago before he met José Mourinho'.

Any good anagrams?

Alper Potuk = Turk pop ale.

Cenk Tosun = Un set conk.

Arda Turan = Tuna radar.

Enes Ünal = Nun lease.

Any songs I can sing if I fancy getting behind them?

There are a few gifts here: They Might Be Giants' 'Istanbul (Not Constantinople)', the Sex Pistols' 'Ankara in the UK' and 'Izmir and My Shadow' by Frank Sinatra and Sammy Davis Jr. On a less intellectual plane we can find Middle of the Road's 'Turkey Turkey Cheep Cheep'.

Our prediction

Last 16

Country / French Equivalent

Croatia / La Croatie

Road to qualification

Croatia nudged ahead of Norway by a single point (after adjustment for racist crowd behaviour) to qualify behind Group H winners Italy, losing only one game in what was potentially a very tricky group. They were also both the group's highest scorers and stingiest conceders.

Tournament history

World cup: 3rd place 1998; European Championship: quarter-finals 1996, 2008.

Manager / Coach

Ante Čačič (Anthony son of Cack). Think Des Lynam on an extremely amateur and ill-disguised witness protection programme. Hats off – in fact, hats inverted – to Ante for his astonishing array of mad surname consonants.

Players to watch

We're going for Mario Mandžukić to rule the roost up-front, but the burgeoning importance of Ivan Rakitić in Barcelona's (post-Xavi) midfield means that we ignore his influence at our peril.

The word on the street

Vanja is in her 40s now and still misses the days of Davor Šuker (she said with a meaningful sigh). Realistically, she's pinning her hopes on Luka Modrić to run the show, a hope shared, she says, by most of the local football writers whose musings she's read. Who are we to contradict her? Except to say that we reckon Modrić will have a quiet tournament and Croatia will come a cropper in the last 16.

Any good lookalikes?

A few, since you ask, mainly in the field of showbiz. Milan Badelj is being encouraged, in the Croatian Comedy Store, to make more of his resemblance to Tony Slattery, while Marko Lešković is actor Andrew Knott, 'Henry' on 1990s cosy Sunday-night drama Where the Heart Is. Andrej Kramarić is an unlikely amalgamation of comedian Lee Evans and Bez from the Happy Mondays.

Any good anagrams?

There is no shortage of footballing jigginess in the Croatian squad in this respect:

Marin Leovac = Cram a love in.

Domagoj Antolić = Mad joint co-goal.

Luka Modrić = Dick L'Amour.

Any songs I can sing if I fancy getting behind them?

'Pula up to the Bumper' by Grace Jones seems like as good a place to start as any other, but fans of pun-infused rock 'n' roll may prefer Bobby Darin's 1958 classic 'Split Splash'. Dubrovnik would nicely fit the scansion of the Specials' 1980 hit 'Do Nothing', but Jerry Dammers hasn't returned our calls.

Our prediction

Last 16

GROUP E

Country / French Equivalent

Belgium / La Belgique

Road to qualification

In Group B, Belgium quite rightly fancied their chances, but could not have predicted that it would be Wales (against whom the 'best team in the world' failed to score – twice) providing toe-to-toe pressure to the bitter end. Both countries qualified with some ease in the final rounds of the campaign, but the experience had been a sobering one for the Belgians. A goals for/against tally of 24/5, notwithstanding the Welsh drought, tells us much about what to expect in the finals.

Tournament history

World Cup: 4th place 1986; European Championship: runners-up 1980.

Manager / Coach

Marc Wilmots (Harvest Resolute Spirit). Following a distinguished playing career, and a rather less notable dabbling in politics, Wilmots has worked his way up the coaching tree to assume control of the national side, doing so with some aplomb. He has long concealed his ire at being considered the 'lost' Kemp brother from Spandau Ballet.

Players to watch

The squad is stuffed both with players familiar to us from their stints in the UK, and with dangerous match-winners: Hazard and De Bruyne will have to be marked extremely closely, while Lukaku and Mirallas have the pace and guile to outwit anyone up-front. We're keeping an eye on Christian Benteke to be the unexpected star of the show, though. The fact that you can probably still name several players we haven't (like the Premier League champions of 2014/15's captain) probably explains how they reached number 1 in FIFA's rankings).

The word on the street

My musical mate Koen states categorically that the Belgians will make at least the semi-finals, and on a good day we reckon he could be right. However, our discussion centres mainly on the strength of his country's defence, which indeed boasts a stingy record in qualification: any backline featuring the likes of Kompany, Alderweireld, Vermaelen and Vertonghen will take some piercing. See, told you!

Any good lookalikes?

The Kevin De Bruyne / Prince Harry thing has been done to death, so we'll begin with Simon Mignolet's gradual realignment as Jeremy Kyle. Steven Defour is another of the embittered 'missing links' from the early days of Boyzone before the line-up was finalised with the two bearded chancers. Jan Vertonghen is reminiscent of a young, more soberly haired Glenn Hoddle, but to suggest there is any genetic link between the two would be wrong. Finally, Jean-François Gillet is defined as 'the smiley rep your kids liked most during your holidays in Lanzarote last year'.

Any good anagrams?

Axel Witsel = Le sex a-wilt or Wilt Sex Ale (which describes most Belgian Trappist beers!)

Nacer Chadli = Nice char lad (eh?).

Dries Mertens = Stirred semen.

Any songs I can sing if I fancy getting behind them?

For sure. You could start with Spandau Ballet's 'BrusselsBound' (noting also the city's honourable mention in Men at Work's seminal 'Down Under'). If you're feeling funky, there's Kool and the Gang's 'Ghent Down on it', Aaliyah's 'Liège Ain't Nothing but a Number', or Madonna's 'Bruges That Girl'. This really is a ridiculous feature, and that's saying something for this book! What next? Adam and the Ants, 'Antwerp Music'!

Our prediction

Quarter-finals

Country / French Equivalent

Italy / L'Italie

Road to qualification

The battle with Norway and Croatia at the top of Group H seemed relentless, but in the end the unbeaten Italians deserved to win the group. A total of 16 goals in ten qualifiers, however, didn't instil much confidence that there's any firepower up-front to be relied on.[8]

Tournament History

World Cup: winners 1934, 1938, 1982, 2006; European Championship: winners 1968.

Manager / Coach

Antonio Conte (Anthony Count). Football aside, Conte has been fortunate to pick up TV and film roles as both 'John Travolta's Italian cousin' and 'John Inverdale's Italian cousin'.

Players to watch

Can Buffon remain as agile and commanding a presence between the sticks as he was at his peak? After 150+ caps, his time must nearly be up, but who's to say he won't play a string of blinders in the Finals? Andrea Pirlo, if fit and selected, still has it within him to change a game, but let's stick our necks on the block here (having wound up my co-author by not mentioning him above) and big up Southampton's Graziano Pellè as a potential match-winner.

The word on the street

Carlo – who is from Perugia but lives in London – is concerned that history may be bearing too heavily on the shoulders of *Gli Azzurri*. Nobody doubts the quality of their

---

[8] This has clearly been put in to check that I've read it as co-author; Graziano Pellè, conqueror of the mighty Maltans, should be mentioned.

players (Italy's Got Talent), and there is experience in their ranks, but Carlo fears the 'X Factor' may be missing. They should be OK in the group, but faced with higher-grade opposition, they could easily be found wanting.

Any good lookalikes?

Mattia Perin played bass in practically every Madchester band, circa 1989-91.

Any good anagrams?

Marco Parolo = Camp loo roar.

Eder = Deer.

Matteo Darmian = A tit named amor.

Any songs I can sing if I fancy getting behind them?

If you're after *fromage cliché*, Dean Martin's 'That's Amore' isn't half as funny as 'Save Your Love' by Renée and Renato. For something a little more meaningful, try Morcheeba's 'Rome Wasn't Built in a Day', or maybe the perennial Dire Straits classic 'Twisting by the Puglia'. Rod Stewart's 'Turin my Heart' may appeal to those watching from afar in Nonquallandia.

Our prediction

Quarter-finals at best.

Country / French Equivalent

Republic of Ireland /
La République d'Irlande

Road to qualification

Their nail-biting play-off seemed to go on forever, but the Republic emerged triumphant over two legs at the expense of Bosnia and Herzegovina. Qualification of any description was a tall order in Group D with Germany and Poland the constant threats at the top, but the boys made it. Cue epic drinking sessions in many houses (including mine).[9]

Tournament history

World Cup: quarter-finals 1990 (sigh)[10]; European Championship: never officially beyond the group stage.

Manager / Coach

Martin O'Neill (Warlike Son of Niall). O'Neill's managerial experience and tactical brain need no explanation, and our feeling is that he'll be able to buoy the lads up sufficiently to get them out of the group, if not necessarily any further this time. Anyone unfamiliar with him facially may

---

[9] But not mine, says the other author.

[10] How you can reminisce about such dull, dull football played by English expats like Townsend and that striker I forget the name of I've no idea! (Tony Cascarino, -Ed.) Just because you've got an Irish passport, you don't have to go all melancholy on the rest of us!

usefully refer to a fifty-something Vinnie Jones stuffed uncomfortably into a suit and glasses and instructed to look uncomfortable in front of the cameras.

Players to watch

Where to start? Let's keep it simple, with some bold predictions: Aiden McGeady will boss the midfield and earn himself lots of sniffing interest from both Barcelona and Bayern Munich; and Jonathan Walters will eclipse Shane Long and Robbie Keane in scoring an improbable number of goals.

The word on the street

Plenty of it. The gist is that everyone's going over for the party and, frankly, anything beyond the group will be a Brucie Bonus. It is widely thought that this will be Robbie Keane's final major tournament, and the hope on the street is that he'll crown his glittering career with something special in front of goal.

Any good lookalikes?

Thanks for asking. Stephen Ward is any bouncer guarding the doors of any nightclub in Leeds, while Richard Keogh is singer Will Young wearing false comedy stubble. Marc Wilson is defined as 'the loveable rogue who reaches the quarter-finals of the *X Factor* every year and ends up doing quite well with bit-part acting and other tasty knock-ons'. Glenn Whelan(sson) should really be playing for Iceland.

Any good anagrams?

Shane Long = Le Shag? Non!

Alex Pearce = Relax Peace

David Meyler = Meady drivel

Any songs I can sing if I fancy getting behind them?

Supergrass kick off proceedings here with a lively rendering of 'Cork by the Fuzz', followed by Pato Banton's 1995 hit 'Dublin Hot'. Kilkenny Rogers can provide strength in depth here, as can Donegal Osmond and A-Laois-A Dixon.

Our prediction

Last 16 and everyone who is a broadcaster will pretend it's not a foreign country.

Country / French Equivalent

Sweden / La Suède

Road to qualification

A Zlatan Ibrahimović double saw off the Danes on aggregate in the play-offs, after the Swedes had finished third in Group G behind Austria and Russia. Some would say they should perhaps have qualified automatically, though.

Tournament history

World Cup: runners-up 1958; European Championship: semi-finals 1992.

Manager / Coach

Erik Hamrén (Autocrat Ham Wren). Hamrén has been at the helm of the Swedish squad since 2009, after notable success at club level throughout Scandinavia. Facially, think Paul O'Grady taking the starring role in a biopic of Gene Wilder.

Players to watch

We're going to say something controversial here: Ibrahimović will not be the star of the show. Goals are more likely to come from Marcus Berg and Ola Toivonen – trust us, we know what we're talking about, though admittedly about other things. We also know that Norwich City's Martin Olsson will score the 'header of the tournament' – it's just a knack we've developed.

The word on the street

I was chatting to Jonas at a Stranglers gig, and he agreed that his country should have qualified automatically. There is, he says, an eerie sense of veneration in the press about the persona of Zlatan Ibrahimović, and it's widely thought that without him (through injury or maverick eleventh-hour retirement) Sweden may be knackered. Like many Swedes, he feels that Andreas Isaksson is indeed immortal and will still be in goal for Euro 2028.

Any good lookalikes?

How dare you suggest 'they all look like Tintin'! It's palpably not true. Robin Olsen, for instance, is Nemanja Vidić gate-crashing an episode of *Lewis* as Kevin Whately's lanky sidekick Hathaway, while Filip Helander is moonlighting as Jordi Cruyff in the mistaken belief that his beard is an effective disguise. Pierre Bengtsson is either (or both) of the blokes from erstwhile X Factor favourites Journey South, while Oscar Lewicki is 92% Morten Harket from A-ha and 8% Graeme Le Saux with a hangover.

Any good anagrams?

Emil Krafth = Filth-maker.

Mikael Lustig = I Like Slut Mag.

Any songs I can sing if I fancy getting behind them?

Plenty of *fromage* available here, from Abba to Roxette and beyond, with Stockholm, Aitken and Waterman also featuring prominently in our musings. We're great fans of John Parr's 'St Malmö's Fire', but save a particular fondness for the Gap Band's 'Oops Uppsala Your Head'. Oh and The Hives are just brilliant (and Swedish).

Our prediction

Last 16 – I hate to say 'I told you so'.

GROUP F

Country / French Equivalent

Portugal / Le Portugal
(ditto re Clouseau voice)

Road to qualification

Got to put their feet up more than most, being in the smallest group with the fewest games. That said, it was tight in Group I with Denmark and (surprisingly) runners-up Albania pushing Cristiano and the boys all the way. Like England the golden generation has departed without tournament success, but expectation is still heaped on those who follow.

Tournament history

World Cup: 3rd place 1966; European Championship: runners-up 2004.

Manager / Coach

Fernando Santos (Ferdinand Saints). Chain-smoking Santos was formerly manager of Greece, whom he took to the quarter-finals of Euro 2012. As well as having the look of a 'tasty' boxing coach from the East End of London, he also serves as a salutary guide to what Manuel Pellegrini could look like if he ever got that absurd coiffure cropped.

Players to watch

It's very predictable to talk about Cristiano Ronaldo all the time, so let's go for Pepe to hold things tight (possibly with a bit of manual persuasion) at the back and Nani to bring his experience to bear in the centre of the park. In addition to the usual suspects, we fancy Virinha to have a decent tournament, and Nélson Oliveira to surprise a few people up front.

The word on the street

We spoke to António from Braga (which means nappy in Spanish), and he confessed that he fears his nation may be too dependent on CR7. Forwards like Cavaleiro and Ukra, he said, have a great future ahead of them, but he wondered whether they shouldn't have been blooded earlier. When pushed for a bottom line, he ruefully concurred with our prediction, despite Ronaldo's capacity to produce mouth-watering, match-changing moments.

Any good lookalikes?

Pepe is Danny from Hear'Say. Nélson Oliveira has recently enrolled as a first-year student at the Danny Dyer Lookalike Academy, and is expected to make great advances over the next few years. His subsidiary subject is 'Retro Gary Birtles'. Cedric Soares looks like he's just started wearing long trousers after a spell in the Infants School.

Any good anagrams?

Bruno Alves = Snob Valuer

Any songs I can sing if I fancy getting behind them?

What better place to start than with Roxette's 'Lisbon to your Heart'? No? Oh, come on, it's better than the 1956 humdinger 'Porto Prince' by Winifred Atwell and Frank Chacksfield. Who? Exactly. OK, can we agree on 'Faro Faro Away' by Slade? If any new Portugal-related songs need to be written for the occasion, Elbow singer Guy Algarvey could be your man.

Our prediction

Last 16

Country / French Equivalent

Iceland / L'Islande

Road to qualification

Iceland emerged from a tricky and buttock-clenchingly tight group, having done battle with the Netherlands (who fell away disastrously) and the Czech Republic (who qualified as winners) at the top, just ahead of best-third-place qualifiers Turkey. For a country with a population as small as Iceland's (comparable to that of Coventry) this achievement should not be underestimated. Qualification was achieved by a clumsy 0-0 draw at home to Kazakhstan, suggesting an England-like ability to turn the simple into a drama.

Tournament history

Prior to 2016, Iceland had never qualified for the finals of a major tournament.

Manager / Coach

At the time of writing, Swede Lars "Lasse" Lagerbäck (Victorious Layer Stream) and Icelander Heimir Hallgrímsson (Homely Son of Stone Helmet) were sharing the role.

Players to watch

There's plenty of experience in the defensive ranks, as well as a few useful newcomers in the backline, such as Magnússon, Hauksson and Eyjólfsson. Cardiff's Aron Gunnarsson is more than capable of directing operations on the bigger stage, and there's a sprinkling of useful goal-scoring contributions from his colleagues in midfield. Inevitably, though, we'll be looking to Kolbeinn SigÞórsson and Alfreð Finnbogason to supply the goals, with what would be a very welcome last-hurrah cameo from Eiður Guðjohnsen if he's feeling up to it.

The word on the street

This was passed on to us third-hand, and apparently came from a bloke called Kris who used to work with the sister of someone we know (full name: Kris Sistersomeoneweknowsson). We couldn't be more specific, but seemingly the guy Kris was very passionate about his footy and saw no great surprise in his country qualifying for Euro 2016. His message – helpfully written in English and without any mad hieroglyphics of the type illustrated above – read as follows: 'Iceland will surprise everybody in the tournament and will reach the quarter-finals'. We'd love that to be the case, but we're being pragmatic in stating that we can't see it happening.

Any good lookalikes?

Aron Gunnarsson bears a passing resemblance to the late Big Country frontman Stuart Adamson, but otherwise most of the squad fall into two sub-branches: the blonder ones are all fruits of the fertile loins of Peter Schmeichel (even though he's Danish and we're obviously implying nothing libellous here), and the mousier-haired ones are the young cousins of Steven Gerrard.

Any good anagrams?

No work required here, as the entire Icelandic squad are anagrams of each other. On me 'ead Sson!

Any songs I can sing if I fancy getting behind them?

Once you've done Björk's back catalogue, pickings get a bit slimmer. Veruca Salt helped us out in 1997 with 'Volcano Girls', in response to Baccara's 'Geysir I Can Boogie', and Department S rounded things off with their seminal 'Is Reykjavik There?'

Our prediction

Group stage exit

Country / French Equivalent

Austria / L'Autriche

Road to qualification

A stingy defensive record was at the heart of Austria's qualification campaign, with only five goals conceded in ten games (the same as second-placed Russia). Their qualifying record was second only to England's. This bodes well for the finals, but can we be sure they've got much to offer up-front?

Tournament history

World Cup: 3rd place 1954; European Championship: first round 2008.

Manager / Coach

Marcel Koller (Marky Rage). Koller bears a passing resemblance to Raúl's uncle Francisco, as well as displaying the gravitas of a number of Portuguese news anchors.

Players to watch

The Austrians haven't got a wealth of goalkeeping experience to draw on, but with the strength of their defence (Fuchs, Prödl, Klein et al) this shouldn't be a problem. Could this be Martin Harnik's moment in midfield? We think so. We're equally confident that this could be Marc Janko's greatest day up-front. You heard it here.

The word on the street

We had a choice of four correspondents in Vienna, the most coherent of whom was Andreas, who contested our prediction (see below), reckoning that with a handful of solid players based in the English leagues (Fuchs and Prödl again, plus Kevin Wimmer, Marko Arnautović, Andreas Weimann and Marco Djuricin – who admittedly plays for Brentford) we should know better than to belittle his compatriots' chances. We consider ourselves duly chided, but are sticking to our guns.

Any good lookalikes?

Much evidence of Liverpudlian interest here: Kevin Wimmer is any Scouse call centre team leader, while his teammate Marcel Sabitzer is cheeky-chappie singer and entertainer Ray Quinn. In wider British issues, Heinz Lindner stoically refuses to accept that he is Gareth Bale's cousin, and there's a touch of the 'Christopher Eccleston as represented in Madame Tussauds waxwork' in Florian Klein.

Any good anagrams?

Marc Janko = Roman Jack.

Robert Almer = Bertram Role.

Marco Djuricin = Iconic Drum Jar.

Any songs I can sing if I fancy getting behind them?

OK, so you're expecting 'Vienna' by Ultravox – and you're welcome to it. You can also have 'Sugar Coated Salzburg' by the Lightning Seeds and 'Graz Entertainment' by the Jam. Non-punning purists can add pretty much anything off the *Sound of Music* soundtrack if they feel the need (though we Edelweiss them not to).

Our prediction

Group stage exit (although if they do manage to win it, Germany will probably put another star on their shirts!)

Country / French Equivalent

Hungary / La Hongrie

Road to qualification

Beating Norway in the play-offs ensured Storck's men would enjoy a run-out at the finals, but they made heavy work of their group, losing out in automatic qualification to Northern Ireland and Romania and then missing the 'third place' route in the most unlikely of twists (see above). Their goals for/against tally in the group hinted at a lot of 1-1 draws to come. The loss of their last group game to Greece was actually irrelevant in context of qualification, but losing to Greece (recently vanquished by the Faroe Islands and Luxembourg) can hardly be good for confidence.

Tournament history

World Cup: runners-up 1938, 1954 (officially robbed); European Championship: 3rd place 1964.

Manager / Coach

Bernd Storck (Strong as a bear Stork). German Storck could easily ply his trade as an enigmatic, slightly maverick detective parachuted inexplicably into a bucolic setting in the South West of England. His career in football management has led him through a series of second-in-command roles at club level, plus the flexing of his national muscles in Kazakhstan before taking the Hungary gig in 2015. Apologies for actually telling you something about the person there, as opposed to oblique, unintelligible references to *Rentaghost* and love children!

Players to watch

Plenty of experience is available to the Hungarians, in the form of veteran goalkeeper Gábor Király, midfield general and beloved Baggie Zoltán Gera, and defenders Roland Juhász and Vilmos Vanczák. We have a sneaky suspicion that, despite the dearth of goals alluded to above, there might be a cheeky spurt from the boots of Ádám Szalai.

The word on the street

We know Tibor through an obscure punk chat forum. He reckons (via Google Translate) that the team will perform solidly and industriously, but without distinguishing themselves. We tend to agree, on the grounds that our Hungarian is less than rudimentary and we don't know any different. I once tried to ask a hotel receptionist in Budapest 'Do you speak English?' I asked in my best Hungarian 48 times to ever more non-plussed looks. Eventually she resorted to, 'I'm sorry, do *you* speak English?'

Any good lookalikes?

Zoltán Stieber joins Austrian Heinz Lindner in the 'Gareth Bale's Extended Family Hall of Fame', which is clearly gathering momentum outside of Wales. Ákos Elek and BBC presenter Matt Baker are twins separated at birth, while Roland Juhász is a young Robson Green doing Robbie Williams during an ill-advised karaoke night.

Any good anagrams?

Zoltán Stieber = Laziest or bent?

Ádám Nagy = Gay ad man.

Dénes Dibusz = Dude Bizness.

Dániel Tözsér = Laziest drone.

Ádám Simon = Mad maison.

Any songs I can sing if I fancy getting behind them?

George Ezra's 'Budapest' and Duran Duran's 'Hungary Like the Wolf' are obvious but enduring choices. Anyone wishing to respect the division of the capital city could tap their feet to David Bowie's 'Buda of Suburbia' and Queen's 'You're my Pest Friend'. Readers with more provincial tastes might look more towards EMF's 'Györ Unbelievable'.

Our prediction

Group stage exit

ON THE BENCH

Country / French Equivalent

Denmark / Le Danemark

Road to Qualification / Prediction

Denmark famously won the tournament in 1992 after failing to qualify, but gaining entry after Yugoslavia fell apart in civil strife. Perhaps all the hype doesn't help teams and, if not, England certainly have an excuse. Anyway this time Ukraine are already fighting each other quite a lot, including conflict with Russian separatists. Turkey borders a war zone. One thing you can confidently predict about international affairs is that it's unpredictable, so the moment any of the qualifiers resembles a fully-fledged war zone, pile all your cash on the Danes.

Group Stage – The Six Groups

	Group A	Group B	Group C
1	France	England	Germany
2	Romania	Russia	Ukraine
3	Albania	Wales	Poland
4	Switzerland	Slovakia	N Ireland

	Group D	Group E	Group F
1	Spain	Belgium	Portugal
2	Czech Rep	Italy	Iceland
3	Turkey	R Ireland	Austria
4	Croatia	Sweden	Hungary

The road to the Final

Prediction à la Tinpot (read the explanation and then enter your prediction in the tables provided)

Whether you are there, or in front of the TV, you will – of course – want to prove your superior predictive skills, yes? And just when you thought this book couldn't give you any more joy, we're proud to bring you exclusive use of the tinpot method. So what is prediction à la Tinpot? Well we could just throw in the fixtures and tell you to predict against your mates. But we're going to give you more. Something you can use over and over again. It's one of the best kept secrets in the world and considered so dangerous that it's banned by the Chinese authorities [Editor: Unlikely but actually true]. I speak, of course, about the 'Tinpot' method, used by literally dozens of mostly non-league, ground-hopping anoraks for at least a few years. Follow the link if you dare to see how sad some people really are: tinpot.co.uk. Tinpot stands for – obviously – Truly Insignificant non-Proper Outfits Trophy. Snappy huh?

In the tinpot method you predict as follows:

England v Germany: England winning at half-time, England to win 5-1

And if you had made this prediction for 1 September 2001 in Munich, you would have scored the following points:

- England winning at half time: 1 point
- Correct result (i.e. England win): 2 points
- Correct 'home' goals (i.e. 1): 1 point
- Correct 'away' goals (i.e. 5): 1 point

So each prediction has a maximum of 5 points available. You could just decide to tot up points over the tournament, predicting before each game. Or for each match you could play against an opponent (us if you've no mates!) and award 3 points for a win and 1 for a draw. For instance, if your opponent had predicted a draw at half-time, and England to win 2-1, they would score 2 points for the correct result and 1 for getting Germany's goals correct. You would have won the match 5-3, have 3 points and a goal difference of +2. In the following example, the match ends as a draw.

Player 1: HT Draw, FT Southampton 8-7 Sunderland

Player 2: HT Southampton, FT Southampton 3-2 Sunderland

Since the correct version was 3-0 to Southampton at half-time and 8-0 at full time, player 1 gets 2 points for a Saints win and 1 point for getting the 8 correct. Player 2 also gets 2 points for the Saints win and for predicting they would be winning at half time. Simples?

Here are the matches on which to predict...obviously further down the line you're going to have to pencil in the matches, perhaps using a highlighter to pick out the qualifiers in the group tables...?

Match	Date	UK Time	Venue	GROUP	Country	Country
1	10/6	8pm	Saint-Denis	A	France	Romania

Scorers:

Match	Date	UK Time	Venue	GROUP	Country	Country
2	11/6	2pm	Lens	A	Albania	Switzerland

Scorers:

Match	Date	UK Time	Venue	GROUP	Country	Country
3	11/6	5pm	Bordeaux	B	Wales	Slovakia

Scorers:

Match	Date	UK Time	Venue	GROUP	Country	Country
4	11/6	8pm	Marseille	B	England	Russia

Scorers:

Match	Date	UK Time	Venue	GROUP	Country	Country
5	12/6	2pm	Paris	D	Turkey	Croatia

Scorers:

Match	Date	UK Time	Venue	GROUP	Country	Country
6	12/6	5pm	Nice	C	Poland	N Ireland

Scorers:

Match	Date	UK Time	Venue	GROUP	Country	Country
7	12/6	8pm	Lille	C	Germany	Ukraine

Scorers:

Match	Date	UK Time	Venue	GROUP	Country	Country
8	13/6	2pm	Toulouse	D	Spain	Czech Rep

Scorers:

Match	Date	UK Time	Venue	GROUP	Country	Country
9	13/6	5pm	Saint-Denis	E	R Ireland	Sweden

Scorers:

Euro 2016

Match	Date	UK Time	Venue	GROUP	Country	Country
10	13/6	8pm	Lyon	E	Belgium	Italy
Scorers:						

Match	Date	UK Time	Venue	GROUP	Country	Country
11	14/6	5pm	Bordeaux	F	Austria	Hungary
Scorers:						

Match	Date	UK Time	Venue	GROUP	Country	Country
12	14/6	8pm	Saint-Etienne	F	Portugal	Iceland
Scorers:						

Match	Date	UK Time	Venue	GROUP	Country	Country
13	15/6	2pm	Lille	B	Russia	Slovakia
Scorers:						

Match	Date	UK Time	Venue	GROUP	Country	Country
14	15/6	5pm	Paris	A	Romania	Switzerland
Scorers:						

Match	Date	UK Time	Venue	GROUP	Country	Country
15	15/6	8pm	Marseille	A	France	Albania
Scorers:						

Match	Date	UK Time	Venue	GROUP	Country	Country
16	16/6	2pm	Lens	B	England	Wales
Scorers:						

Match	Date	UK Time	Venue	GROUP	Country	Country
17	16/6	5pm	Lyon	C	Ukraine	N Ireland
Scorers:						

Match	Date	UK Time	Venue	GROUP	Country	Country
18	16/6	8pm	Saint-Denis	C	Germany	Poland
Scorers:						

Match	Date	UK Time	Venue	GROUP	Country	Country
19	17/6	2pm	Toulouse	E	Italy	Sweden
Scorers:						

Match	Date	UK Time	Venue	GROUP	Country	Country
20	17/6	5pm	Saint-Etienne	D	Czech Rep	Croatia
Scorers:						

Match	Date	UK Time	Venue	GROUP	Country	Country
21	17/6	8pm	Nice	D	Spain	Turkey
Scorers:						

Match	Date	UK Time	Venue	GROUP	Country	Country
22	18/6	2pm	Bordeaux	E	Belgium	R Ireland
Scorers:						

Match	Date	UK Time	Venue	GROUP	Country	Country
23	18/6	5pm	Marseille	F	Iceland	Hungary
Scorers:						

Match	Date	UK Time	Venue	GROUP	Country	Country
24	18/6	8pm	Paris	F	Portugal	Austria
Scorers:						

Match	Date	UK Time	Venue	GROUP	Country	Country
25	19/6	8pm	Lyon	A	Romania	Albania

Scorers:

Match	Date	UK Time	Venue	GROUP	Country	Country
26	19/6	8pm	Lille	A	Switzerland	France

Scorers:

Match	Date	UK Time	Venue	GROUP	Country	Country
27	20/6	8pm	Toulouse	B	Russia	Wales

Scorers:

Match	Date	UK Time	Venue	GROUP	Country	Country
28	20/6	8pm	Saint-Etienne	B	Slovakia	England

Scorers:

Match	Date	UK Time	Venue	GROUP	Country	Country
29	21/6	5pm	Marseille	C	Ukraine	Poland

Scorers:

Euro 2016

Match	Date	UK Time	Venue	GROUP	Country	Country
30	21/6	5pm	Paris	C	N Ireland	Germany

Scorers:

Match	Date	UK Time	Venue	GROUP	Country	Country
31	21/6	8pm	Lens	D	Czech Rep	Turkey

Scorers:

Match	Date	UK Time	Venue	GROUP	Country	Country
32	21/6	8pm	Bordeaux	D	Croatia	Spain

Scorers:

Match	Date	UK Time	Venue	GROUP	Country	Country
33	22/6	5pm	Saint-Denis	F	Iceland	Austria

Scorers:

Match	Date	UK Time	Venue	GROUP	Country	Country
34	22/6	5pm	Lyon	F	Hungary	Portugal

Scorers:

Match	Date	UK Time	Venue	GROUP	Country	Country
35	22/6	8pm	Lille	**E**	Italy	R Ireland
Scorers:						

Match	Date	UK Time	Venue	GROUP	Country	Country
36	22/6	8pm	Nice	**E**	Sweden	Belgium
Scorers:						

Group Stage Fixtures – by Group

GROUP A

Match	Date	UK Time	Venue	GROUP	Country	Country
1	10/6	8pm	Saint-Denis	A	France	Romania

Scorers:

Match	Date	UK Time	Venue	GROUP	Country	Country
2	11/6	2pm	Lens	A	Albania	Switzerland

Scorers:

Match	Date	UK Time	Venue	GROUP	Country	Country
14	15/6	5pm	Paris	A	Romania	Switzerland

Scorers:

Match	Date	UK Time	Venue	GROUP	Country	Country
15	15/6	8pm	Marseille	A	France	Albania

Scorers:

Match	Date	UK Time	Venue	GROUP	Country	Country
25	19/6	8pm	Lyon	A	Romania	Albania
Scorers:						

Match	Date	UK Time	Venue	GROUP	Country	Country
26	19/6	8pm	Lille	A	Switzerland	France
Scorers:						

GROUP B

Match	Date	UK Time	Venue	GROUP	Country	Country
3	11/6	5pm	Bordeaux	B	Wales	Slovakia
Scorers:						

Match	Date	UK Time	Venue	GROUP	Country	Country
4	11/6	8pm	Marseille	B	England	Russia
Scorers:						

Match	Date	UK Time	Venue	GROUP	Country	Country
13	15/6	2pm	Lille	B	Russia	Slovakia

Scorers:

Match	Date	UK Time	Venue	GROUP	Country	Country
16	16/6	2pm	Lens	B	England	Wales

Scorers:

Match	Date	UK Time	Venue	GROUP	Country	Country
27	20/6	8pm	Toulouse	B	Russia	Wales

Scorers:

Match	Date	UK Time	Venue	GROUP	Country	Country
28	20/6	8pm	Saint-Etienne	B	Slovakia	England

Scorers:

GROUP C

Match	Date	UK Time	Venue	GROUP	Country	Country
6	12/6	5pm	Nice	C	Poland	N Ireland

Scorers:

Match	Date	UK Time	Venue	GROUP	Country	Country
7	12/6	8pm	Lille	C	Germany	Ukraine

Scorers:

Match	Date	UK Time	Venue	GROUP	Country	Country
17	16/6	5pm	Lyon	C	Ukraine	N Ireland

Scorers:

Match	Date	UK Time	Venue	GROUP	Country	Country
18	16/6	8pm	Saint-Denis	C	Germany	Poland

Scorers:

Euro 2016

Match	Date	UK Time	Venue	GROUP	Country	Country
29	21/6	5pm	Marseille	**C**	Ukraine	Poland

Scorers:

Match	Date	UK Time	Venue	GROUP	Country	Country
30	21/6	5pm	Paris	**C**	N Ireland	Germany

Scorers:

GROUP D

Match	Date	UK Time	Venue	GROUP	Country	Country
5	12/6	2pm	Paris	**D**	Turkey	Croatia

Scorers:

Match	Date	UK Time	Venue	GROUP	Country	Country
8	13/6	2pm	Toulouse	**D**	Spain	Czech Rep

Scorers:

Match	Date	UK Time	Venue	GROUP	Country	Country
20	17/6	5pm	Saint-Etienne	D	Czech Rep	Croatia
Scorers:						

Match	Date	UK Time	Venue	GROUP	Country	Country
21	17/6	8pm	Nice	D	Spain	Turkey
Scorers:						

Match	Date	UK Time	Venue	GROUP	Country	Country
31	21/6	8pm	Lens	D	Czech Rep	Turkey
Scorers:						

Match	Date	UK Time	Venue	GROUP	Country	Country
32	21/6	8pm	Bordeaux	D	Croatia	Spain
Scorers:						

GROUP E

Match	Date	UK Time	Venue	GROUP	Country	Country
9	13/6	5pm	Saint-Denis	E	R Ireland	Sweden

Scorers:

Match	Date	UK Time	Venue	GROUP	Country	Country
10	13/6	8pm	Lyon	E	Belgium	Italy

Scorers:

Match	Date	UK Time	Venue	GROUP	Country	Country
19	17/6	2pm	Toulouse	E	Italy	Sweden

Scorers:

Match	Date	UK Time	Venue	GROUP	Country	Country
22	18/6	2pm	Bordeaux	E	Belgium	R Ireland

Scorers:

Match	Date	UK Time	Venue	GROUP	Country	Country
35	22/6	8pm	Lille	E	Italy	R Ireland
Scorers:						

Match	Date	UK Time	Venue	GROUP	Country	Country
36	22/6	8pm	Nice	E	Sweden	Belgium
Scorers:						

GROUP F

Match	Date	UK Time	Venue	GROUP	Country	Country
11	14/6	5pm	Bordeaux	F	Austria	Hungary
Scorers:						

Match	Date	UK Time	Venue	GROUP	Country	Country
12	14/6	8pm	Saint-Etienne	F	Portugal	Iceland
Scorers:						

Match	Date	UK Time	Venue	GROUP	Country	Country
23	18/6	5pm	Marseille	F	Iceland	Hungary

Scorers:

Match	Date	UK Time	Venue	GROUP	Country	Country
24	18/6	8pm	Paris	E	Portugal	Austria

Scorers:

Match	Date	UK Time	Venue	GROUP	Country	Country
33	22/6	5pm	Saint-Denis	F	Iceland	Austria

Scorers:

Match	Date	UK Time	Venue	GROUP	Country	Country
34	22/6	5pm	Lyon	F	Hungary	Portugal

Scorers:

Group Stage – Final Tables

GROUP A									
Country	Pd	W	D	L	GF	GA	GD	Pts	Qualification Status
1									Q
2									Q
3									Q?
4									

GROUP B									
Country	Pd	W	D	L	GF	GA	GD	Pts	Qualification Status
1									Q
2									Q
3									Q?
4									

GROUP C									
Country	Pd	W	D	L	GF	GA	GD	Pts	Qualification Status
1									Q
2									Q
3									Q?
4									

GROUP D									
	Country	Pd	W	D	L	GF	GA	GD	Pts	Qualification Status
1										Q
2										Q
3										Q?
4										

GROUP E									
	Country	Pd	W	D	L	GF	GA	GD	Pts	Qualification Status
1										Q
2										Q
3										Q?
4										

GROUP F									
	Country	Pd	W	D	L	GF	GA	GD	Pts	Qualification Status
1										Q
2										Q
3										Q?
4										

Round of 16

RU A v RU C

Match	Date	UK Time	Venue	Country	Country
37	25/6	2pm	Saint-Etienne		
Scorers:					

Win B v 3rd A/C/D

Match	Date	UK Time	Venue	Country	Country
38	25/6	5pm	Paris		
Scorers:					

Win D v 3rd B/E/F

Match	Date	UK Time	Venue	Country	Country
39	25/6	8pm	Lens		
Scorers:					

Win A v 3rd C/D/E

Match	Date	UK Time	Venue	Country	Country
40	26/6	2pm	Lyon		
Scorers:					

Win C v 3rd A/B/F

Match	Date	UK Time	Venue	Country	Country
41	26/6	5pm	Lille		
Scorers:					

Win F v RU E

Match	Date	UK Time	Venue	Country	Country
42	26/6	8pm	Toulouse		
Scorers:					

Win E v RU D

Match	Date	UK Time	Venue	Country	Country
43	27/6	5pm	Saint-Denis		
Scorers:					

RU B v RU F

Match	Date	UK Time	Venue	Country	Country
44	27/6	8pm	Nice		
Scorers:					

Quarter - Finals

Win R16 (St Etienne) v Win R16 (Lens)

Match	Date	UK Time	Venue	Country	Country
45	30/6	8pm	Marseille		
Scorers:					

Win R16 (Paris) v Win R16 (Toulouse)

Match	Date	UK Time	Venue	Country	Country
46	1/7	8pm	Lille		
Scorers:					

Win R16 (Lille) v Win R16 (St Denis)

Match	Date	UK Time	Venue	Country	Country
47	2/7	8pm	Bordeaux		
Scorers:					

Win R16 (Lyon) v Win R16 (Nice)

Match	Date	UK Time	Venue	Country	Country
48	3/7	8pm	Saint-Denis		
Scorers:					

Euro 2016

Semi - Finals

Win QF (Marseille) v Win QF (Lille)

Match	Date	UK Time	Venue	Country	Country
49	6/7	8pm	Lyon		
Scorers:					

Win QF (Bordeaux) v Win QF (St Denis)

Match	Date	UK Time	Venue	Country	Country
50	7/7	8pm	Marseille		
Scorers:					

Final

Win SF (Lyon) v Win SF (Marseille)

Match	Date	UK Time	Venue	Country	Country
51	10/7	8pm	Saint-Denis		
Scorers:					

Venues and locals

Lille, Stade Pierre-Mauroy	(50,186)
St Denis, Stade de France	(81,338)
Lyon, Stade des LumiEres	(59,286)
Saint Etienne, Stade Geoffroy-Guichard	(41,965)
Marseille, Stade VElodrome	(67,394)
Nice, Allianz Riviera	(35,624)
Toulouse, Stadium Municipal	(33,300)
Bordeaux, Nouveau Stade de Bordeaux	(42,115)
Paris, Parc des Princes	(47,000)
Lens, Stade Bollaert-Delelis	(38,223)

This guide can only have whetted your appetite for the tournament, if not for reading, and you must be itching to sally forth, singing 'tally bally ho' and 'Rule Britannia' as you go. But for those of you for whom it has been a venture into 'literature' a mite longer than you're used to, here below is the very, very, extremely quick guide to what to expect.

(And I should start by saying that this has been provided by a resident of France and his French *amis*, such that anything that smacks of casual parochialism is, in fact, casual national bigotry of a sort.)

City	Best Known For
Bordeaux	Wine, money, snobbery
Inhabitants	
Rich (wine-soaked) snobs	

City	Best Known For
Lens	Poverty, violence, football, mining (deceased), hatred of people from Lille. A tiny town of only 30,000 inhabitants and yet incredibly every single one of them supports the football team and goes to every home game.

Inhabitants

Loveable and passionate, working class, salt-of-the-earth people. One of only two real football teams in France. Speakers of Ch'tis, a largely incomprehensible form of French, now rendered famous and loveable in a Hollywood-style feel-good movie called 'Welcome to the land of the ch'tis'. Here is a link to the film which shows the funny bits (obviously there aren't many):

https://www.youtube.com/watch?v=fY5cWL4SUmw.

Only in France would it constitute being called a comedy, although apparently it is being remade in Hollywood as I type this sentence.

City	Best Known For
Lille	Beautiful and classic 19th Century French city surrounded by slums and Islamic Jihadi groups. Gateway to the continent etc. Known for a cruel indifference towards people from Lens.

Inhabitants

The friendliest most affable people I have ever met. Also known to speak Ch'tis, a largely incomprehensible version of French. Compensated for by their sheer bonhomie.

City	Best Known For
Lyon	The other Paris. The other Paris commune (failed) started by the anarchist Bakunin. Materials and fabrics, if you are into that kind of thing.

Inhabitants
Think they are the 'real France' yawnzzzzz. In practice this means they are highly susceptible to supporting right-wing nationalist parties and the WW2 Vichy regime that were sub-contracted by Hitler... [not an uncontroversial view]

City	Best Known For
Marseille	Criminals, beaches, the sun, corruption and the mafia (Ed: Is that not covered by criminals and corruption?)

Inhabitants
Generally regarded as the rudest and most uncivil people in France. And as you can imagine that is a hotly contested title.

City	Best Known For
Nice	Too rich by half, though Agnès Varda made a lovely documentary about the Côte d'Azur which almost redeems it. But not quite. Here is a free link to the documentary: http://www.dailymotion.com/video/xd0vho_du-cote-de-la-cote-agnes-varda-1958_shortfilms

Inhabitants
Rich, effete, decadent. If only I had the money to join them.

City	Best Known For
Paris	The Paris commune, the French Revolution, a police force that murders Algerians and throws their bodies into the Seine or crushes them to death on the metro and then the whole country pretends it didn't happen. Yes, Paris has a rich and diverse history.

Inhabitants

Despite the haughty, arrogant and snobbish demeanour of many Parisians (not the ones in the *banlieues*, though) they are in fact deeply insecure about themselves. Like all French people, monkeys in zoos and little children, they hate to be mocked and laughed at or to make a fool of themselves in public. Fans of Paris Saint-Germain (themselves well known racists and fascist sympathisers) unfurled a now legendary banner to visiting supporters of Lens saying 'Paedophiles, Unemployed, and the Inbred - *Welcome* to Ch'ti Land.' In Freudian terms this is best understood as a form of 'displacement' whereby the patient (Parisians) projects their own characteristics onto other people. In fact only Belgium has a deeper commitment to such practices than Parisians. [Again, not uncontroversial!]

City	Best Known For
Saint-Denis	No-one knows where this is. No-one cares. Possibly a song title by Blondie. (Ed: Far be it from me to correct our esteemed author and his collection of co-authoring loonies, but Saint-Denis is home to the Stade de France and so home to the final, one suspects!)

Inhabitants

No-one knows anyone who lives there.

(Ed: Although this is possibly true; Wikipedia lists a small list of French sounding non-entities from Saint-Denis, but none of them you've ever heard of!)

City	Best Known For
Saint-Etienne	Home of the only other team in France and for English football fans one of the two glamour teams of the 1970s along with Ajax. Remember how exciting they were: Platini (before he became a horrible little fat bastard), Rocheteau, Tigana, and all the others. Marvellous stuff but roundly mocked by French football fans for their claims to have been robbed of the European Cup by Bayern Munich and Glasgow's famous flat, not round, crossbars, which saw the ball fail to bounce over the line. Yet another reason not to visit Scotland. Look it up yourself, it's on YouTube, I can't be bothered. City is a bit like Lens, only less attractive.

Inhabitants

Like Lens, a tiny working-class industrial town full of tough blokes and real football fans who make a noise at games. Very un-French.

City	Best Known For
Toulouse	A Pink City, hated by many French people for being full of foreigners and therefore not really French. Home to the French inter-galactic space agency and generally very pretty. Feels Mediterranean.

Inhabitants

They like rugby a lot down here so imagine it to be a bit like one of the many shit towns in Surrey but with better weather and architecture. I haven't actually tested that theory but suspect it to be true.

And below, for those requiring a little more detail and balance - Voilà! (which is French for "tough luck – this is what you're getting, *mes amis!*")

Bordeaux

Whilst the summary above may get to the nub of things, Bordeaux is really jolly nice. Lots of monuments and buildings (only Paris has more in France) mean that UNESCO bestows official 'jolly nice' status upon it. Around a quarter of a million people live here and if you were just wanting to soak up the atmos of Euro 2016 you could do much worse. Until recently it was home to one of only 3 'real tennis' courts remaining in France (most perished in all that anti-aristo stuff, circa 1789) but they inexplicably knocked it down. I could tell you a lot more about how jolly nice it is but I'm thinking of going there myself, and as much as possible want to discourage the riff-raff (oui, c'est vous).

Possibly true fact: Home of Vinexpo, the world's largest wine exhibition/conference thing.

Lens

Look up Lens via the internet and you'll find much less than you will about Bordeaux. Trip Advisor offer lots of indoor shots and other available photos seem to have been taken out of focus or from a considerable distance. It looks OK out of focus and/or from a considerable distance, but I'm still thinking Bordeaux's for me. Lens was largely destroyed in World War One and is close to Vimy Ridge, which is particularly significant to Canadians for the efforts of their soldiers there. The Canadian National Memorial is worth a visit and moment of quiet contemplation lest you take these nationalistic championships too seriously. UNESCO status: unacknowledged.

Possibly true fact: Lens has France's highest levels of pollution, with levels of garlic eight times the EU's safe limit.

Lille

Lille is in French Flanders, near the Belgian border, and so also with the handy Flemish name "Rijssel" which is not at all confusingly different if you're heading here by car from Belgium. In matters of food and booze, Lille definitely errs on the side of the Belgian, so if big bowls of chips, steak and beer are your things, this may suit more than the nouvelle cuisine and cheeky Chablis of elsewhere. Louis Pasteur was from Lille and it is twinned with Leeds as well as with towns in Israel (Haifa) *and* the area administered by the Palestinian Authority (Nablus). It's also a kinda railway hub, so if your journey is taking you through it anyway, do get off and eat some chips. Pourquoi pas?!

Possibly true fact: Founded around 640 AD as the city of L'Isle.

Lyon

It has a slick website of its own called 'Only Lyon' which is available in English and extols the virtues of Lyon as a city to visit at any time of year. Greater Lyon is more than 2 million strong, making it France's second largest urban area. Like Bordeaux it makes UNESCO's official list of jolly nice places to look at, and has a national and international reputation for its cooking with local delicacies both weird and wonderful. Oddly it is twinned with Birmingham, although they were perhaps going with the 'choose places that make us look good' idea since Beirut is also on the list. Allegedly Roman Emperor Claudius was from here; and also Jean Michel Jarre, well-known peddler of electronic lift music.

Possibly true fact: Candidate city for European Lift Music Convention, 2027.

Marseille

Probably safe to say this is not the prettiest place compared to much of southern France. Or compared to all of France. Or Europe. Or anywhere really. Except perhaps Coventry and Portsmouth. That said, the climate is nice and it had a proper tart-up (I think that's the technical term, from the French verb *tarter*[1]) for European City of Culture status in 2013. Its location means that Marseille has been something of a gateway city to France and it has a diverse population including a large Algerian minority. Zinedine Zidane is from here. Twinned with Glasgow, where presumably 'Zizou' learned his head-based greeting which lost France the 2006 World Cup.

Possibly true fact: This is where Chris Waddle murdered the French language in 1989ish.

Nice

Unlike Bordeaux, Lens, Lille, Lyon and Marseille, I've actually been to this one. Curiously, my memories of it as a 22-year-old are not much different from that of Swanage as a 10-year-old; although 1976 was a particularly hot

---

[1] The verb *tarter* actually means 'to hit', -Ed.

summer I'm sure that can't be right, and certainly the food in Nice was a far cry from crab-paste-and-sand sandwiches, and a tad more expensive. Nice is another place with its own website but not as nice as Lyon's is. About the same size as Southampton, it is considerably nicer and that may not be entirely a climate thing. Twinned with Edinburgh; so Marseille/Glasgow, Nice/Edinburgh feels about right. Well that's told you bugger all, hasn't it?!

Possibly true fact: Hop on a further ferry here and end up in Corsica.

Paris

And I've been here too, the last time being during the Rugby World Cup final of 2007. Royally pissed off (or should that be Republically pissed off?) that France wasn't in the final, the public transport system was brought to a halt by sulking strikers, but that didn't stop us playing jenga under the Eiffel Tower as England were robbed by the TMO (IMO). OK, OK, South Africa were also better. Palaces. Touristy stuff. Being English is a crime. Not speaking French is a crime. Being English and trying to speak French is a crime. Pissing in the street is *not* a crime. Do you really need a guide? I'd prefer to go to Lens, I think.

Possibly true fact: Public urination is legal. And whilst that might not be quite true, read the footnote![2]

---

[2] I tried to prove this one by typing into a search engine "number of people charged with public urination in Paris in the last 2000 years" and to my surprise I read about Monsieur Rebete: M. Rebete is a special agent in Paris's war on public urination. Part of an elite, 88-member force called the Brigade des Incivilites, M. Rebete scours the streets for all sorts of boorish offenders. Dressed in civilian clothes and driving an unmarked car, he tickets everyone from litterbugs to people handing out unauthorized flyers to Parisians who don't pick

Saint-Denis

All that stuff above about Paris plus a Basilica (where most French kings were buried when they did that sort of thing) and the Stade de France. Twinned with Coatbridge (home of Albion Rovers). Marseille/Glasgow, Nice/Edinburgh, Saint Denis/Coatbridge – all makes sense. Industrial heritage, lots of communist mayors historically. Most famous for England's first European Championship finals win in July 2016.

Possibly true fact: Debbie Harry had a crush on the place.

Saint-Etienne

On the road twixt Lyon and Toulouse. Famous for its once decent football team; a Rot Weiss Essen or Huddersfield Town of France if you will, although at the time of writing actually riding high in Ligue 1 once again. Twinned with Coventry. Oh dear, oh dear; says it all.

Possibly true fact: I cannot even think of anything to make up; making up tosh can be a tremendous strain, you know.

---

up after their dog. But what the French call urine sauvage, which translates to "wild piss" is the hardest to crack. While France's capital has campaigned with some success to have Parisians pick up after their pets, the city is still struggling with the presence of pipi. Urine is hard to escape in certain parts of the city, be it on the street, in the Metro or in parks. Members of the Brigade say there is no high season for urinary offences, but summertime heat heightens the stench. City hygiene workers scrub down and spray tens of thousands of square metres of walls and pavements every month. But according to M. Rebete, a former sanitation worker himself, the products they use - a combination of disinfectant and deodorizer, blasted through a hose with hot water - are no match for the streams that seep into the city's stone streets. (Wall (presumably urine soaked) Street Journal, 1 September, 2009)

Toulouse

A solid rugby town of around a million people and after Paris, Lyon and Marseille, the 4th largest agglomeration in France. In 1814 it was the site of one of the major battles of the Napoleonic Wars and today bits of it have made UNESCO's jolly nice list. The locals go by the name of 'Tossers' and the City is twinned with Portsmouth. No, no, of course that's not true but I'm way beyond bored with this padding lark now. Look, it looks nice. Most of France is, really. And it will be warm. And they only pretend to hate the English and in fact respect us all deeply. So be it with England, the Tartan Army, Welsh warriors or massed hordes of 'Northern Ireland Nil' – just go and enjoy. What have you to lose?

Possibly true fact: It has a massive town hall which closely resembles Buckingham Palace.

Conclusions:

GO ON! Hop on the ferry (you know you want to)

This is pretty much the only part of this book we've been able to write once the finals draw was made. It could well mean that what we write below, hurriedly and to meet the terms of the book contract, contradicts (if you look closely) some of our earlier predictions. Please don't look too closely or we'll send the boys round. We hope you've enjoyed the book, and will indulge us one last time as we offer our gut reactions and pick out the games which we'll be glued to. As with much football, the anticipation and the sense of possibility is probably the best part.

Group A – C'est pas un fix!

Tournaments need a certain amount of home success to work well as was demonstrated by the 2015 rugby world cup. Nowhere is this more so than in France where the supporters are so fickle that they score even more highly than Notts Forest fans on my imaginary fickle-o-meter.

Fortunately, France have already won the Euros and World Cup at home something which I don't believe has been done by any other country and may yet be the key this time. They will be delighted with the draw this time, which rather than Italy, Turkey and a number of other group stage nasties has offered up Albania (currently top of the group on alphabetical order), Romania and Switzerland. Given that 4 third placed teams get through, if France don't make it to the last 16 we can expect a collective shrug big enough to set off a Tsunami in New York. Not really a group where the phrase 'Group of Death' (Le groupe de la mort) has any place, although we're not predicting (m) any goals in the games not involving France, so it could be deadly dull. A weak enough group that Albania might just achieve in excess of their official co-efficient and horrendous historical record.

Group B

The way the draw has shaped up, it is entirely possible that England v Wales could be a match to determine which one goes through to the round of 16 as group winners, or conversely that the loser might already be eliminated. I'm not saying either way, except that the last time I saw an England v Wales game the English froze (Rugby World Cup) and in the last football match the England players looked like the proverbial 'many circuses and wigwams' (much too tense). Suffice it to say it's the second match and pivotal and might be the match of death (or death match). If England finish bottom of the group, Roy will be out on his ear. If they win it, he'll not get any credit. Looking at the group I have a sneaking suspicion (well more of a hope really) that Russia finishes bottom. Nothing against them or anything of course; apart, that is, from the serial invading of neighbours, repression and assassination, and macho, homophobic culture epitomised in the form of its dictatorial leader. [Ed: Perhaps we'd better edit that bit out? I'm not keen on polonium for breakfast]

Group C – Die Todesgruppe

Group of death? You've gotta be kidding. The boys in green can handle those three minnows, no bother. Look what the other boys in green did to Germany in the qualifying group…

I think we can take it as a given that Germany will win the group – even when they're coasting, there's more than enough big-tournament savvy for them to keep their wits about them and cobble together enough points to top out comfortably. Poland should have learned their lessons from qualifying, and are likely to be tough to beat – they'll be looking to hold Germany and win their other two games, going through as runners-up.

Northern Ireland will have their sights set on beating Ukraine – which is eminently achievable – doing their damnedest to get something out of the Polish game and hoping to catch Germany on the break.

The format of the group stage – with much store set by finishing as strongly as possible in third place, to go through as one of the four best in this position – opens doors of possibility for both Irelands and, realistically, this is going to be the ticket to the North's success.

We've said plenty elsewhere in the book about their spirit and work ethic, but also about their organisation. They have it within them to create a major shock if they can hold their nerve – nobody will care if progression is achieved by means of a dull 0-0 draw against Germany on 21 June in Paris.

Did we mention daring to dream? Let's do it.

Group D – El grupo de la muerte

This is a strange one. Spain are odds-on favourites to stroll through this group, but what happens beneath them is anyone's guess. Including ours. So, not for the first time in this book, here's some confident-sounding guesswork, backed up by robust psychology and an even more robust *rioja*.

I've got an uneasy suspicion that this may end up being the closest – and possibly the dullest – of the six groups, crammed with low-scoring draws, and possibly decided on goal difference, head-to-heads and other such shenanigans.

There was a certain solidity in the qualifying patterns of the Czech Republic, Croatia and Turkey, the latter being consistent enough to qualify as the strongest third-placed nation. But who will step up to the plate in the finals?

The smart money will be on the Czechs to finish second behind the Spanish. They've played some good, attacking football, and they're simply better organised – and have greater strength in depth in their squad – than the other two nations.

On a more positive note, it will be up to Spain to show the watching world that they've recovered from their humiliation in the 2014 World Cup in Brazil. Their squad and abilities are not in question, but can they show the necessary bottle on the big stage? We're sure they can, and are confident not only that they'll win the tournament, but also that they'll create a *fiesta de fútbol* in doing so. You heard it here.

Group E – De Dodengroep / Le groupe de la mort

In whichever of their national languages the Belgians contemplate their grouping with Italy, the Republic of Ireland and Sweden, even they will have to concede that it really is the toughest of the lot.

It's a peculiar group. Belgium are riding high in the FIFA rankings, but many people have an uneasy feeling in their stomachs that the Belgian squad is not yet the finished article, continuing to punch above its weight without really setting the world alight. Witness how well Wales did against them in qualifying. Do we really see Belgium as a force akin to the Brazil of yesteryear, the Spain of recent years, or the Germany of most years? I think they can be matched.

Irish radio took a jauntily bullish tack in analysing the group straight after the draw was made back in December. The Swedes, it was said, were unimpressive in edging past the Danes in the play-offs, and the Irish should have nothing to fear there. The problem with the Italians, it was further asserted, is that they can't score goals – however strong their famed defence may be, they'll need to notch a couple of victories in order to progress. How would it be if the 'biggies' kept drawing with each other and the Irish slipped through on the blind side with a couple of cheeky 1-0s?

Our message is clear: don't be daunted. Yes, it's the group of death, but as rank outsiders the pressure is off the Irish. Recent form has shown that they can hold their own at this level, so let's keep dreaming!

Group F

O grupo da morte? Well possibly. In historical terms all these teams need a break, but many many will shy away from supporting Portugal because of Ronaldo (C) whose comparison of football and slavery might be regarded as distasteful and who loves himself just a bit too much. Picking cotton, whippings, lynchings and rape by the master would not have been any more palatable even with a salary running into hundreds of thousands of dollars. Talking of right wing, Hungary has lurched in that direction recently, a far cry from the progressive ambitions of 1956 and all that; still in football terms many will hope that this football mad nation does something which would make Puskas proud. Austria had a fantastic qualifying campaign and should get out of the group. Iceland (population around the size of Coventry, but considerably happier) are unlikely to lose all their matches and may edge the not so mighty Magyars into 4th. Incidentally, it has been a strategy of this book to poke fun at anyone and everything in order to get a cheap laugh - but I do mean it about Coventry. No seriously... it's an extraordinary place, with a smoothly operating ring road and probably the most southerly properly left wing place in England outside London, but it's still Coventry. Well, there you have it. Can England win? (or Wales or

Irelands?) Well, fortunately, I suspect few people will read this after the tournament so let us ignore the poo-poo of Professor Pierre's French friends and say yes, we can. Greece did! And, besides, I believe in miracles! At the time of writing, football is overshadowed by atrocity in Paris. England have set appropriate expectations of the tournament by losing 2-0 in Spain. Meanwhile a great new era of Greek football has dawned with an away game in Luxembourg. They lost 1-0 of course.

Quick Quiz

(or another avenue for poking the Scottish and Greek 'bears')

So, you've read the book and now you're as near to being an expert as anyone could be after consuming a diet consisting entirely of jingoistic poppycock and codswallop, so here's a quiz:

1. Which team qualified first for Euro 2016 apart from the French hosts?

2. True or False: There are undiscovered tribes in the Peruvian jungle who predicted Scottish non-qualification

3. True or False: But they didn't foresee the rise of Wales, Albania, Iceland and NINIL

4. England beat San Marino 5-0 and 6-0 but what would the scores have been if all San Marino's shots on target had gone in?

5. Against which team did Wayne Rooney beat Sir Bobby Charlton's all time England goal-scoring record?

6. Who said: *Pressure? What pressure? Pressure is poor people in the world trying to feed their families. Working from dawn till dusk just to feed their young. There is no pressure in football?*

7. True or False: Germany were amongst the top three nations in qualifying in terms of average home attendance.

8. England's average crowd was nearly 75,000. If England had achieved the same proportion of the population crowds as the Faroe Islands did, what would their average crowd have been?

9. Which of the following had the lowest average crowd in qualifying: Greece, Cyprus or Albania

10. Which team scored the fewest goals whilst successfully qualifying?

11. True or false? England conceded fewest goals in qualifying

12. Can you name the four undefeated sides in qualifying?

13. Which was the only side that didn't qualify automatically or reach the play-offs to concede fewer than 10 goals?

14. Gibraltar scored against Scotland (obviously). Against which team did their other goal come?

15. Which bottom-placed team in qualifying had the most points of all bottom-placed teams?

ANSWERS

1. England
2. True
3. True
4. 5-1 and 6-1
5. Switzerland
6. José Mourinho, proving that he doesn't talk absolute cobblers the whole time
7. False: They finished more than 20,000 below England, more than 5,000 below Poland and 1,000 fewer than Scotland
8. Approximately 4 million
9. Greece
10. Albania with 10, although playing in a group with only 5 teams
11. False, England and Spain both conceded 3 but Romania only 2
12. Austria, England, Italy and Romania
13. Estonia with 9
14. Poland, although losing 8-0 at the time
15. That was the proud boast of Greece with 6 points

Helpful Phrases

(unhelpfully translated – i.e. possibly inaccurately, we can't tell - by someone whose specialist language is Spanish)

English	French
Could I introduce you please, to a lump of cheddar cheese?	Puis-je vous présenter à un gros morceau de Cheddar? (fromage Chedderoise?)
We're going to score one more than you!	Nous allons marquer un but de plus que vous!
I am the Lord Mayor of Rotherham (no not Rozzer'am)	Je suis le Maire de Rotherham (non, pas de Rozzer'am)
Bon Appétit!	Good appetite!
Yes, I'm fluent in French; tell me your views on continental philosophy	Oui, je parle couramment le français; donnez-moi votre opinion sur la philosophie continentale
Yes, I'm fluent in French; tell me your views on different varieties of olives	Oui, je parle couramment le français; donnez-moi votre opinion sur les différentes sortes d'olives
Yes, I'm fluent in French; tell me your views on which wines to eat with horse/snails/frog's legs	Oui, je parle couramment le français; quel vin me conseilleriez-vous pour accompagner du cheval / des escargots / des cuisses de grenouilles?

English	French
Whatever you may have heard, in England it's the North-Easterners who are the most sophisticated	Contrairement à ce que vous auriez pu entendre, en Angleterre ce sont les gens du nord-est qui sont les plus raffinés
Where is Hull exactly? Towards the end of the 19th Century my dear fellow	Où est Hull, exactement ? Vers la fin du siècle 19, mon cher
I'm as happy as Frenchman who's invented a pair of self-removing trousers (copyright: E. Blackadder)	Je suis aussi heureux qu'un Français qui a inventé un pantalon qui s'enlève tout seul (copyright: E. Blackadder)

About the Authors

Lloyd Pettiford

Lloyd was born in Manchester and has borne a grudge against the place ever since, remembering his early life there as cold, grey and uninspiring; it's changed so much. Childhood talent and enthusiasm soon gave way to lazy cynicism and a career in his beloved specialism of bureaucratic routines. His CV includes a spell with NASA as space suit tailor and Dulwich Hamlet Reserves as a penalty-taking left back. He doesn't like cats and feels most comfortable when writing complete gibberish, especially about football. He once beat Scott Barratt from the penalty spot for North Staffs Poly to win 3-2 against Stoke City (reserves who were available on the Poly finals night)[1].

Ronan Fitzsimons

Ronan was born in Newcastle upon Tyne. His career in football peaked in 1979, when he led the mighty Shincliffe

---

[1] He's never missed a penalty, but unlike his co-author is much too modest to mention it.

Youth Club to victory in the Durham County Youth Club Cup, scoring the winning goal in the final. Things tailed off thereafter, although he does hold the distinction of never having missed a penalty (are you reading, Matt le Tiss?). He now juggles a sensible day job with a secondary career writing books on topics as diverse as punk rock, football and Spanish grammar. As a counterpoint to Lloyd's 'gibberish', Ronan prefers 'a surreal take on the truth'.

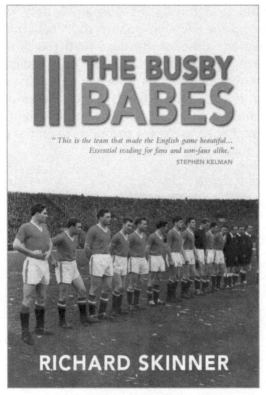

£8.99, ISBN 9781910692578

'More than merely an account of a tragedy, it is a portrait of an era and a tribute to a group of young men; working class heroes all whose talent, endeavour and camaraderie transcends football. This is the team that made the English game beautiful, and to rediscover this golden generation is to revisit the foundation, the death, and the rebirth of something magical. Essential reading for fans and non-fans alike.'

Stephen Kelman, author of *Pigeon English*